THE END

WHEN THE LAST STAR HAS FALLEN

JIM BUSHONG

SonLife Ministries
P.O. Box 404, Lovingston, VA 22949

Printed in the United States of America.

ISBN
979-8-88945-216-4 (Paperback)
979-8-88945-217-1 (eBook)

Brilliant Books Literary
137 Forest Park Lane Thomasville
North Carolina 27360 USA

The Promise

The earth will be completely laid
waste and totally plundered.

The Lord has spoken this word.

The earth dries up and withers, the
world languishes and withers, the
exalted of the earth languish.

The earth is defiled by its people;
they have disobeyed the laws,
violated the statutes and broken
the everlasting covenant.

Therefore a curse consumes the
earth; its people must bear their guilt.

Therefore earth's inhabitants are
burned up, and very few are left.
ISAIAH 24:3-6

In loving memory of my husband...

CONTENTS

Looking Forward

Looking Back

The Future

The Millennium Covenant

Eternal Life

AUTHOR'S COMMENTS

As you look at the United States, are you at all disturbed with the direction this country has taken over the last twenty-five years? We have watched a society that has become so self-centered that it is very difficult to identify the difference between us and Europe and many other countries of the world that are self-defined as Socialist. People from these countries have flocked to the United States to escape socialism. Now they find themselves living in a country quickly becoming like those they fled.

When you look around the globe, can you see the desperate situations that nearly every country, especially those in the Middle East and North Africa, are experiencing? None of this should be a surprise to those who follow the prophecy of the Bible. You do not want to be uninformed of what is surely coming as the world draws nearer to what God has warned us about. This study of the book of Revelation will answer many of your concerns.

Where do we see God in our society? Over the years we have removed the Ten Commandments from the walls of our public schools and government buildings. God has been under assault for many years now, to the point where we can only find Him in the closets or basements of these same buildings. History has shown us that when God lifts His hand from a nation, that nation does not survive. We are in serious trouble here and around the world as we live by a code of "situational ethics" rather than the ethics of God. The time has come to look back and learn the lessons of history, because history will indeed repeat itself. We have angered God and He will take revenge in a most horrific way. There is little time left to ignore the coming of God's Wrath.

INTRODUCTION

It is important to look over the past centuries from a Biblical perspective to help us put the book of Revelation into context. The first three chapters of Genesis are a great example of how Scripture is written. In the first chapter of Genesis, God gives us an overview on how the world was created. We know what was created on each day and how the Lord felt about His creation. However, there were special events that took place during the creation of this world and of man himself. The wonders that took place during the creation would indeed take more time to explain. In the second and third chapters, the Lord takes us through creation again, but includes more specific details of the event. Many questions would go unanswered if God had not added these details of the creation sequence. The first three chapters of Genesis compliment and complete each other in the account of our beginning.

The book of Revelation is written in a similar fashion. Just as God wants us to know how our world began, He wants us to know how it will end, and to know where we are in that process. The Revelation will show us how the advent of Christ places us right in the middle of God's plan for His children.

I sincerely believe that your life will be impacted when you complete this study. The best way to use this commentary is to open your Bible to The Book of Revelation and read along with the indicated verses. We will be discussing some issues that people find very complex. You will quickly learn that the Revelation of Christ Jesus is not hard to understand. Without a doubt, there are some questions that cannot be answered right now, but we will know all the answers when we are with Jesus. If you choose to read only the commentary under the assigned text, you will miss much of what the Holy Spirit can teach you as you study the End Time of this world. By reading the appropriate Bible verses, you will discover what Jesus wants you to know about His return.

<u>Definition(s)</u>:

End Time: This is a span of time leading up to the seven years of Tribulation. It is important to remember that the end time can also be described as the time you have left at the end of your life here on this earth. Both of these options are unforeseen.

Related Verse / *<u>1 Thessalonians 5:1-3</u>…Now, brothers, about times and dates we do not need to write to you, for you know very well that the day of the Lord will come like a thief in the night. While people are saying, "Peace and safety," destruction will come on them suddenly, as labor pains on a pregnant woman, and they will not escape.*

Last Days: The Last Days can be associated with the life span of any human being on this earth. The Last Days always refers to a time leading up to the end of life whether it is the end of our natural life or the End Time of this world as described in 2 Timothy 3:1-5.

The time is coming, and indeed may already be here, as witnessed by the actions of many radical people as they demonstrate their desire to eliminate all Christians around the world. This is especially true in Israel and the United States, which is an indicator of the beginning of the end of this world. As we look at our neighbors both next door and around the world, we are seeing power hungry countries that will stop at nothing to overpower the people on earth with their ideas of how to live. We are at a point now where treacherous men will use any means to gain power. The real tragedy of these events is that the average person believes that this trouble is reversible. Our question should be: has this situation been foretold by the Creator of the world; thus making it irreversible?

More has been written about the Revelation of Jesus the Christ than any other book of the Bible. Revelation can be hard to read and even more difficult to understand. First, the book of Revelation is not written in chronological order. The writer begins to tell a story, and right in the middle of an event, John moves to a different subject. That is why this book must be read at a time you have deliberately set aside to use this Bible study. Do not get discouraged because you do not understand everything you read the first time. Read it over a few times before coming to any conclusions.

Most of you have formed your own opinions about Revelation issues by listening to your pastor, priest, bishop, etc. Whatever they say about the book, you say "amen" and go on to tell the story just as you heard it from your church leaders. Revelation is one book that you cannot have someone else tell you what it says. You <u>must read it yourself</u> and understand most of what God is telling you. Of course, some areas leave us wondering what message Christ is conveying to us. In that case, we must accept the fact that the message is unclear at this moment and go on. The Holy Spirit may open up your heart to those issues as you mature in the Lord. Your church leadership may say something that will trigger an answer to your question.

The Holy Spirit living within us yearns for our souls to know what Jesus is saying about His return in the book of Revelation. We see many commentaries today that have been written which stray far from what Jesus is telling us in His Revelation. Many studies by spiritual leaders in the church say, *"I think what Jesus meant by this is,"* when describing a particular event. When they do that, they risk their opinion being one hundred and eighty degrees opposite of what Jesus meant. I will admit it is tempting to add more to the story, but we MUST remain true to the text and accept what Jesus is telling us through the Holy Spirit. That is why it is very important to understand what Jesus is saying to us and to recognize the warning signs as the Tribulation period approaches. The Tribulation may come at any time from minutes to years, but we must understand that it WILL come at the appointed time.

All of us have questions about the book of Revelation. Many people look to this book for answers to the questions about what happens to us after death. For example, is there life after death? Is there a literal heaven and hell, and what are they like? If there is life after death, what must I do to obtain that life? What will the end of this world be like and when will it happen? Can we do anything to survive the so-called "Apocalypse?" Will there be a world, as we know it, after all the disasters described in Revelation have decimated the world God created? All of the answers to these questions are in the Bible, the book we will be reading. Remember, <u>all</u> are guaranteed to live eternally. The huge question that only you can answer is this: where will <u>you</u> spend eternity?

When we are done with this study, you will be able to answer the hard questions of Revelation. You will know what your role is as a member of the family of Christ in the End Times. Your anxiety level will be decreased significantly and your confidence in your salvation will be strengthened. You will have much to learn after this experience, but you will be equipped to study deeply into the more complex issues of Revelation.

Looking into the future is a subject that has fascinated us since the beginning of time. Even in our advanced technical world, some people still rely on horoscopes, fortunetellers, palm readers, and psychics. We anxiously await the predictions of a New Year. What will happen to the leaders of our country? What kind of trouble will the famous people in our society get into this year? How many tornadoes will strike and where? How many hurricanes will hit the United States? What will our weather be tomorrow and how will our plans be affected by that weather? We worry little about today, but work ourselves into a paranoid frenzy about tomorrow. We wring our hands and imagine all sorts of wild and weird things. Yet, if we would only read what Jesus has to say about the future, our fears would be replaced by peace.

Matthew 6:34 tell us not to worry about tomorrow. Christ is always there for us, so when we feel anxiety beginning to take over, we must remember that worrying will not add one single hour to our lives and the problem is not larger than our God. If we will only learn to take our problems to the Lord and leave them in His hands, we will have more peace in our lives and less uncertainty.

Luke 12:25, 26...*Can worrying about life add a single hour to our existence? Since you cannot do this very little thing, why do you worry about the circumstances of life?*

The Bible is filled with prophesy, most of which has been fulfilled. (And before this thought is lost, let me remind you that fulfilled prophecy is proof that the Bible is indeed the word of God). Some suggest that there are no prophets in our time. But that is not what God says. Prophecy is a gift promised to His church, by God through Christ Jesus and the Holy Spirit, along with other gifts. As you study the Scriptures, you will find yourself learning things that you will want to share with others. When you share what you have learned with others, it can be prophecy to their ears.

Related Verse(s) 1 Corinthians 14:1…Follow the way of *love and eagerly desire spiritual gifts, especially the gift of prophecy.*

Prophecy is <u>not about something new</u> on the horizon, but it is an <u>interpretation of the writings of the Holy Scriptures</u> (The Bible). The gift of prophecy is still alive today in the family of God. We experience true prophets and, of course, we experience false prophets. The Apostle Paul in <u>I Corinthians 12:7</u> talks about this gift: *Now to each one the manifestation of the Spirit is given for the common good. To one there is given through the Spirit the message of wisdom, to another, miraculous powers, to <u>another prophecy</u>.* Paul addressed the various gifts of the Spirit given to the church, one of which is the gift of prophecy. Most of us rarely think about using the gift of prophecy in our own churches. It could be that there is no one in your church with that gift. However, your pastor is often in a prophetic mode. Prophecy is a subject that does not get discussed often. Prophesying means taking on a huge risk for the person making a prophetic announcement. In most churches, he or she could be laughed out of the congregation. Anyone who would dare approach the church leaders with a declaration that he or she thought God had given them a prophetic word for the church could possibly be banished from that church, literally or figuratively.

Let's be clear about prophecy. No one can come up with anything in the realm of prophecy unless it comes from the Holy Spirit through Scriptures. In the New Covenant, God does not speak to man directly, but through the Scriptures. Man can get in enough trouble just by interpreting the Bible (2 Peter 1:20-21).

Biblical prophecy is specifically for the church (1 Corinthians 14:22) *"prophecy however, is for **Believers**,"* but many denominations avoid or discourage this gift as if it were the plague. Prophets can be men or women who have something to share with us that confirms our relationship with the Godhead. Being fair, prophecy has also damaged some churches beyond repair. A prophet does not exercise authority over those to whom he or she is speaking. They are merely conveying their interpretation concerning the word of the Lord as they feel it has been given to them. To <u>accept</u> their prophecy as <u>truth</u>, we must search the

Scriptures and pray earnestly. That concept is true of this commentary as well.

Related Verse(s) I Corinthians 14:1...*Follow the way of love and eagerly desire spiritual gifts, <u>especially the gift of prophecy</u>.*

The problem with most modern day prophets is that, just as the prophets of old, their prophecies must be true. Any so-called prophet, who sets dates for the return of Jesus, is not a prophet. Matthew 24:36... *No one knows about that day or hour, not even the angels in heaven, nor the Son, but only the Father.* If they tell us of something else in the future different than Biblical truth, we should not accept their word. There is no room for a prophet to be wrong. Once prophecy has been given, it MUST be fulfilled as written in the Scriptures. We have experienced several of these self-appointed prophets in our time that abused the word of God by setting dates for the return of Christ, only to see that date come and go. To make matters worse, they continued to set other times and dates until they looked silly, and were forced to stop setting dates. However, men, and women still follow these false prophets to this very day. Men or women claiming to be prophets of the Lord MUST be right every time they give us prophecy. Prophecy today, of course, is the public interpretation of Biblical writings as they apply to our life as Believers. Nothing new is going to happen to us that is not written in the Scriptures. That means that Scripture drives prophecy. It is very easy to be deceived by something that is not Biblically based.

In 1 Thessalonians 2:2, we read about an early church that was already having problems with false prophets. In this case, the false prophets were saying that Messiah had already come. No person can come up with a prophecy that is not specifically inspired by the Holy Spirit through the Word of God. It is important that we look very closely at the context of what has been written about Christ Jesus and His return for the church. The Apostle Paul tells this church that the day of the return of Jesus will not happen until the antichrist has been revealed for who he is, and that will not happen until the Mid-Tribulation point. It is extremely important that we read the book of Revelation carefully and critically.

Jesus prayed for us in John 17:15, asking His Father to protect us from evil. There has been, and always will be, evil in various forms to deceive the church; causing many in the pews to leave the security of

Christ and those He has put around them to give them support. False prophets come to us looking very well qualified to speak of the words of God; but their real goal is to get Christians to reject the true Christ and accept a false god.

Many people are so apathetic about the return of Christ that they are willing to believe anything that comes from the pulpits concerning this book of prophecy, and are satisfied that the end times will be just as their church leaders have stated. Others are so frustrated with the modern day prophecy about the return of Christ that they have abandoned their faith. Still others are looking to these modern day prophets for answers to the big question; when will Christ return to take us out of this world so we won't have to suffer the perils of the Tribulation? What you will read in this study is based on the truth of Scripture. It has not been written to be popular nor does it assume you are too stupid to learn what the Holy Spirit is saying concerning the return of Christ Jesus.

Today we are experiencing an ever-increasing interest in the secular community concerning what the Bible has to say about the events described in the book of Revelation. Billions of dollars have been made from book sales that attempt to put a spin on God's word. It is critical for today's "Born-Again" Believer to read and understand what Christ is telling each one of us concerning the events of the last seven years of this earth. We must remember that just because an author sells millions of books, it does not mean that the information inside is true. In fact, the authors of a recent series of books addressing the End Times state that their books are written as fiction. The goal of Christ is not to leave us in confusion about His return, nor does He want us to rewrite the Scriptures on this topic. As you read The Revelation of Christ Jesus with complete obedience to the Holy Spirit, you will be able to discern the "last days" events and prepare accordingly.

It will be helpful to remember that the events described by John in this book are from his perspective as a first-century Christian. We will be reading of weird looking creatures with many eyes and heads that in the mind's eye appear to be gross and offensive. John will describe certain creatures that will test our ability to think in the deepest form of the abstract as we try to identify some of the beings. Some of the things he will say to us cannot be explained. However, when you finish this study you will be able to form a clearer picture of what the Harvesting of the Saints and the Second Coming of Christ entail, and how they will affect your life. You will feel a sense of urgency to relate what you have learned to others in the church and especially those in your family. I would caution you to be ready to defend what the Holy Spirit has taught you and stand firm in your decision to follow Him through all that lies ahead.

Before we look at the immense destruction that will come upon our world, we need to look closely at what is happening in the world today. One of the things that concern our world leaders the most is that smaller countries now pose the same threat in the area of weapons of mass destruction as the larger ones once did. When we look into the future, we can see it is possible that we are about to enter the End Time of the world. When we take into account the environmental issues, infectious diseases, famines, catastrophic events, and cowardly acts perpetrated on innocent civilians by radical Islamic terrorists, it can be overwhelming. As we focus on the role of the church in End Times, and how the events will unfold, Revelation will become easier to read and understand. You will come to understand what your role should be during these end times.

I would urge you not to get too deeply engrossed in the explanation of how many toes, eyes, and horns some living things may have in this book. Put things that you do not yet understand aside, and wait until they fit into the overall picture of Jesus' message. We will get into the deeper explanations of issues and complex events as we continue through the study. Do not give up early. Keep reading even though it may seem very confusing for you.

This study will take you through a step-by-step process. It is more important to discover how we should be living our lives as Christians during the last days than trying to unfold complex issues. The church has a definite role to play in the End Times, and we are getting closer to those days. I encourage you to become a Revelation prophet in your church community.

THE GREAT DECEPTION

The Great Chaos

In this commentary, the Great Chaos refers to a time when all the nations of the world are in immense financial and political disarray. Many countries have collapsed financially, including some significant ones. There will be a great outcry for a new one-world order making way for a one-world religion. This has happened before with other great societies in various regions of the world. Leading up to the "End Time," the entire world will be in chaos and looking for a one-world leader to save them.

I believe that we can agree as we look around the world, we find ourselves in terrible trouble. Nation after nation has overthrown their past leadership, and new radical groups have replaced the old regimes. Chaos has caused countries to frantically look for reasonable leadership while other factions look to stop any form of democracy. The United States has reached a point that we now allow people to take over government buildings, parks, and even our streets. I understand that some of these statements can sound as if panic is about to follow, but I must tell you that the world appears to be in a state of chaos. I am not saying that the "sky is falling," but I am saying it has begun to fall.

During the end of time, the "Great Chaos" will make people distrusting of their neighbors and even their own families. Believers will be hated so much that even their children will be responsible for turning their parents in to the government for worshipping God.

According to Matthew 24:9-11, we will see such terrible times that result in Believers being handed over to local government agencies to be persecuted even to the point of death. At this very moment in time, the United States is the number two target of Islamic terrorists to be completely wiped out. Israel is number one on the list for eradication. Look at what we see today. Every Islamic country around Israel is now in agreement that Israel is their main enemy and must be wiped off the map.

Sleeper terrorist cells have infiltrated every country on earth and will wreak havoc on the civilized world when told to do so. Schools, churches, shopping centers, sporting events, and synagogues will be targets for small nuclear weapons that will be delivered by women and children with these weapons of mass destruction under their clothing or in other inconspicuous ways. People will live in fear as they try to move about without putting themselves at risk. They will even feel uncomfortable in their homes. The economy will be in shambles with no hope of a quick recovery. No target will be considered off limits to these horrible people. The borders of the United States will be compromised more than they already are and the country will be nearing collapse. Now, of course, you can say that this is just speculation, but in your heart, you know that this description has crossed your mind many times. You should listen to that wee small voice telling you that serious trouble is on the horizon.

The president and his staff will have to govern from the Situation Room in the deepest part of the White House or even worse, from an undisclosed bunker somewhere. Local governments will break down and their citizens will be exhausted from the unsettled times. When combined with natural calamities such as earthquakes, drought, famines, hurricanes, tornadoes, and the like, people will begin to look for a leader who will be able to restore order to their part of the world. Two things will begin to happen as the world comes to understand the enormous trouble they are experiencing. One sector of the population will be looking for a strong leader, a savior, so to speak. The other sector will be looking to be raptured out of the world and into the arms of Christ, where they would be spared the continuing chaos and persecution. Only one of those things will happen at this time!

There will be a man who will say all the right things, perform all the right tricks in the form of miracles and wonders, and who will promise to restore peace out of chaos and re-establish worldwide tranquility. He will be accepted by most without reservation. The Christian society will accept him as a representative from God Himself. The people of the world will sweep this man into power; and for three and a half years live in relative peace and tranquility. Most of the world will be satisfied. The Believers of the world will recognize this fellow as the prophesized antichrist and begin their plan for The End. Part of our plan will be looking for those Believers who failed to be prepared for this time.

For a time, the antichrist will perform a well-rehearsed deception that will prove to be the beginning of the end for this world. Even the Middle East will be quiet and filled with optimism when this man brokers a peace agreement between the nations of the Middle East and Israel. In early 2013, we see no hope for the conflict in the Middle East. Who would ever think that just one man could come along and mesmerize the Arab people to the point that they would allow Israel to rebuild their Temple in the same place where the Dome of the Rock stands today? The unfortunate fact is that there is a man coming on the scene very shortly who will demonstrate his power and influence by radically changing three countries that are in the midst of chaos, and offer solutions that change these three countries into an historical time of peace and safety that has never been known in this area. He will perform verifiable miracles and show the world his great power by calling fire from heaven as a sign that he is from God or God himself (Daniel 11:36).

Over the years we have seen men in leadership roles that looked good and sounded good for our country. The Apostle Paul told us of a man who will not only look the part of a great leader, but will be a man who has extreme power. Those people who do not believe in the Son of God will fall in love with the antichrist. The average citizens of the world will be amazed at what they will be seeing as the antichrist performs unbelievable miracles that will compare with what Jesus did when He was on this earth and stun the world's population. II Thessalonians 2:11 says that God will send a powerful delusion on those believing the lie told to them by the evil representative of Satan.

Then something will happen that will bring the world back to its knees. After three and a half years of the sporadic peaceful leadership of the antichrist, peace will be replaced with turmoil. The world will be the target of the One who created it. Great torment, never before experienced by man, will result in this world being destroyed. The man who formed a one-world system is finally identified as "The Antichrist" as the False Prophet orders the entire world to worship an image of the evil antichrist that stands in a wing of the Temple of God (Revelation 13:11-12). What follows is a description of the world during the next three and a half years.

As we look back after, the worldwide religious atrocity of what is called "The Pre-Tribulation Rapture" of the church will be exposed as Christians by the hundreds of thousands will turn their backs on their Salvation and lose their trust in the Christ of God due to the artificial false promises of the evil antichrist. We will lose up to one-third of active church members (stars) when they follow the antichrist as he performs miracles, even calling fire down from heaven. They were told they would leave this world before Jesus began to pour out His judgments on the earth's population that turned their backs on Him, but this rapture will not happen as they were told (Rev. 12:4).

One-third of the church of Christ will take the Mark of the Beast that brands them into an evil membership that will lead to their souls being thrown into the Lake of Burning Sulfur for eternity. They will scream and cry out to God asking for mercy, but mercy left them when they took on the Mark of belonging to Satan without thinking about the truth of Scripture. The excuse that they did not know this would happen and that their religious leaders told them they would escape all of the Tribulation will be found to be a lie. The Scriptures told them about the end of days and what would be the future for those who would reject the Truth.

The Bible warned of this day, but Bible reading is not very popular in these last days. What we teach those entrusted to our care should be examined very carefully and align with the Word of God. This Bible study will expose the deception of the so-called Pre-Tribulation Rapture event. The sad thing about this terrible deception is that it will cause millions of church members to be lost forever with no hope of reversing their error.

Related Verses / <u>Matthew 24:10-13</u>…*At that time many will <u>turn away from the faith</u> and <u>will betray and hate each other</u>, and many false prophets will appear and deceive many people. Because of the increase of wickedness, the love of <u>most</u> will grow cold, but he who <u>stands firm</u> to the end <u>will be saved</u>.*

This commentary will be challenging to those who read it. Its message is not popular and will be rejected by a majority of readers, but it is nevertheless the truth from the Word of God. There is no doubt that the Pre- Tribulation Rapture event has been a great moneymaker for some. There have been thousands of books written about the event and even a series of books explaining what might happen afterward. The money made by this hoax has been a boon to local churches and national ministries. Woe to those who preach and teach the things that cause people to sin and walk away from Christ. Such things must come, but woe to the men through whom they come. Those who teach the Pre- Tribulation Rapture of the church prior to the Second Coming of Christ are teachers in error of the truth and should tremble when thinking of what they are doing to those who follow them. The Bible addresses these men and women in 1 John 4:1-3.

The risk for the average Believer during the times of chaos will be that a man is coming on the scene that will make every other charismatic man appear insignificant when compared to him. This man will be the antichrist. Those who follow the antichrist thinking that he is from God will lose their position in the family of Christ. You can confirm this by reading Matthew 7:21-23 as Jesus speaks of those who talk the talk, but refuse to walk the walk. In other words, some Believers are like the wind that blows from one direction, only to change one hundred and eighty degrees in the other direction in the blink of an eye.

Religious leaders do not understand that their teachings will last far beyond their years here on earth. Because of the failure of family members to pass down the building blocks of Scripture to other family members, some of these spiritual leaders may be off the hook because their previous memberships have passed on. There are thousands of pastors teaching this evil Pre-Tribulation Rapture assumption right now, and it will be extremely difficult to change minds even after they see the truth in the Scriptures. If you have been told for forty years that you will be spared any persecution in the Tribulation and then you discover that you were being lied to; I would hope you would search Scripture and confirm the Truth for yourself right away. It will be too late if you continue to keep moving forward with your eyes closed.

There is a good chance that the church you belong to teaches this view. Let me make this very clear, here and now; we are not to break fellowship with those who hold this Pre-Tribulation Rapture view. It is not my place or yours to judge anyone. However, we are to stand ready to give support to our brothers and sisters who will be tempted to follow the antichrist. This commentary was written to show us how to stand with those who find themselves very confused about what is happening around them in the last days.

It is up to each one of us individually to use Scripture to prove all things written about the subject of the return of Christ to this earth. It would be wonderful if preachers and teachers would see the error of their ways and tell the church that they were wrong. This will not happen, of course, because they would lose billions of dollars in contributions. Their pride and pocketbooks will never let them reverse their assumptions. **Woe** to those ministers who continue to place money and reputation over the well being of those in their care.

THE GREAT TEACHER

The Birth Pains

We forget sometimes that Jesus came to earth not only to die for our sins, but also to minister to us. He spent hours upon hours teaching us about Himself and the Kingdom of God. We can be assured that nothing major concerning Him, His Father, or the Holy Spirit was left out of His ministry.

If He was talking about sin, we know exactly how to define the original sin and how to identify other sin in our lives. Jesus taught extensively about morality and left no doubt as to how we are to conduct ourselves as His children. When questions arose about when and how to pray, He left us several examples; most notably what is referred to as "The Lord's Prayer." He made sure we would know in detail how to become witnesses for Him. Whenever the question of His return for His Church occurred, He left no doubt about the method and timing of that return. That is not to say that He gave the specific day and time, because He did not know. Only God, His Father in heaven, knows the details. So why do we have so many theories concerning the return of Jesus for His saints?

Let's look at why Christ Jesus made sure that an entire book of the Bible would be written about the Harvesting of the Saints and His Second Coming. As we go through this study, I will naturally question events that are not specifically written about in this book, yet are often taught as if they were. For example, if Jesus did not mention the raising up of the church prior to the Tribulation, then we have to assume that any Pre-Tribulation Rapture event has to be conjecture. Jesus would not conceal the truth from us. Christ has given us a simple explanation for His return. Just as a side note here; I cannot find a verse in any Bible that mentions a pre-tribulation rapture event without having to modify the verse or link it to another verse unrelated to the return of Christ; nor can I find any theologian that will state that there is one such verse. In all fairness, an argument for a Mid-Tribulation Rapture can be based on some verses taken alone. However, there is no Scriptural evidence for a Pre-Tribulation Rapture.

The Pre-Tribulation Rapture could be viewed as the Creator of this world sneaking halfway back to earth to take some or all of His church home. That would mean that people left here on earth would have to guess what was going on as millions of men, women, and children magically disappear from the earth. I can tell you that there is no way the Creator of this earth would leave any doubt about what was happening as He harvests His church from an evil world. I will identify the evil teaching of a Pre-Tribulation Rapture theory by going back in history.

You will read for yourself the first mention of a pre-tribulation rapture event written by an ill teenage girl in Scotland in the year 1830 (See Appendix A). When looking further back in history we read nothing about this event. We do read below of Lazarus, a close friend of Jesus who died. In fact, he had been dead for several days before Jesus arrived. Jesus' friend was dead for so long his body began to have a foul odor. Jesus called out his name. Lazarus walked out of the burial cave he was in, and the miracle was complete. He exited the grave to live with his family for a predetermined time before he would die. Lazarus' sister had been distraught when Jesus did not arrive for several days. As Jesus walked up to her, He said, *"Your brother <u>will rise again</u>." Martha answered, "I know he will rise again in <u>the resurrection at the last day</u>"* (John 11:23).

Now, let's look at another aspect of this conversation. If there was to be a pre-tribulation rapture event of some sort, and Jesus did not inform Martha of this event, He would have been guilty of withholding the truth, and I know of no one that would accuse Jesus of such an offense. If we were to take what Martha said at face value, it would be a better argument for a Post-Tribulation Rapture event. It is very important that we look carefully at what Jesus is saying and read His words critically.

Again, we must understand that this would be a perfect place for Jesus to show us an example of the Pre-Tribulation Rapture. He did not choose to do that. We should have serious doubts about any rapture event other than the one spoken about in Chapter Fourteen of Revelation. This story must make you think twice about any coming of Christ other than what is written in the Revelation of Jesus.

In Revelation 14:14-16, an angel is described as sitting on a cloud dressed as one looking like a Son of Man. This was an angel who was preparing to harvest the church for Christ Jesus. We know this to be an angel because of the following verse saying, *"then another angel came out of the Temple."* The second angel told the angel who looked like a son of man to take his sickle and harvest the saints of Christ.

We are told of this earlier in the Book of Mark. He said that Christ would send His angels and gather the Believers from the four corners of the earth. The story in Mark debunks the fable that Jesus will come to earth to rescue His saints from the Tribulation. In fact, the angels of heaven will gather the saints to meet Jesus in the clouds and then go on to heaven waiting for the Wrath of God to be completed (Mark 13:27).

As we get into the study of the book of Revelation, I want to go over the questions the disciples had for Jesus about the End Times and His Second Coming. Jesus' entire ministry on earth was focused on teaching us about His love for the entire world and the fact that He would return one day to redeem His church. He was the Messiah that the nation of Israel had been waiting for, but Israel never recognized Him as such. Because Israel did not accept Jesus for what He was, the Gentiles were given the opportunity to accept Him and they have by the millions.

Isaiah explained to us the thoughts of God as they related to the nation of Israel not understanding who Jesus was, or for that matter, who their God was. In Chapter 6:9 of Isaiah, God explained their calloused heart for God. He said these people (Jews) would hear the voice of Christ, but never understand Him. They would see the Messiah, but never perceive Him. Then our time would come to see, hear, and understand the saving grace of the Messiah.

Jesus made it very clear that the salvation He offered would be made available to the Gentile population of the world. The time would come that salvation would be offered to the entire world, no matter what the cultural or ethnic background. Christ Jesus is a Jew and He makes no apologies for His favorite and chosen people, the Jews.

Actually, when we accept Christ as our personal Savior, we become grafted into the Jewish nation. Adopted, yes, but we are still sons and daughters of the King. He ushered in a period of time for the Gentiles (The Church Age), when non-Jews can take advantage of His love and accept His offer to spend eternity with Him.

In Chapter 11 of the Book of Romans we read an explanation of how we Gentiles are grafted into the family of God. The author of Romans, who by the way was guided by the Holy Spirit, used a tree as an example. Many Jews walked away from God, not to return until after the events of the "Last Days" are over. They had the opportunity to experience the gift of the Spirit of God in their lives. Gentiles were given the opportunity to take the positions left open by the ones leaving the security of God. By faith, we accept God and His Son through the Holy Spirit who is now in us.

Jesus has given us a special privilege, along with God the Father, to be part of their family. How wonderful it is that we, who are not God's chosen people, are awarded that opportunity through a special process called "Grace." If you have accepted the Son of God, that is Christ Jesus, then you are in the family of God with all the rights and privileges it offers.

Jesus was asked three important questions in His earthly ministry by the disciples concerning when He would return for His church. The early churches were always asking Paul and other Apostles about when Christ would return. We will see that even back then, the Second Coming of Christ was an important issue for the church. Many false theories had been bantered about and the church was as confused then as it is today (2 Thessalonians 1:3).

Our best strategy is to find out exactly what Jesus was talking about with His disciples, and what His answers were to the questions about the Second Coming. Then we will discuss issues brought up by the early church. Notice, one more time, Jesus speaks of only coming to earth <u>one more time</u> and that is referred to as the Second Coming of Christ.

We will begin by looking at the three questions His disciples were asking in Matthew 24:3… *As Jesus was sitting on the Mount of Olives, the disciples came to him privately. "Tell us," they said, "when will this happen, and what will be the sign of your coming and of the end of the age?"*

Jesus explained that there would be specific signs before the End of the Age, and that certain things MUST happen before He returned for His church. I have heard people say, "Jesus could come at any time" or "If the rapture doesn't happen before then" when referring to an event in the near future. These statements are erroneous and basically call Jesus a liar! He was quite clear in His responses to the apostles when they asked about these things. The events He described to them at this time and in future talks revealed things that are set to happen at an exact time and in a set order. Of course, all of this was once again explained to John in Revelation. These things cannot be changed or altered. We can be assured that they will happen.

Jesus tells us many times to "be prepared" to meet Him. We may not live to see the great day of His return to reign on earth, but we WILL see him at our death, which can come at any time without any warning. As believers, we know that our last breath here on earth is followed in less than a nanosecond by our next breath in the Paradise of God. Many will miss this experience because of their arrogance.

THE FOLLOWING IS A COMMENTARY ON THE QUESTIONS ASKED BY THE DISCIPLES OF CHRIST

Matthew 24:3-24

Question 1. WHEN WILL THIS HAPPEN?

Answer: Matthew 24:36…*No one knows about that day or hour, not even the angels in heaven, not the Son, but only the Father.*

Jesus is very specific about no one knowing the day and hour that has been appointed by His Father for the coming of the Son, Jesus. Jesus will not return until the day set by the Father in heaven. He cannot return anytime He wishes. The day of the Son's return to Harvest His church has been set in stone. What God promises, He will do. We can beg and pray for this date to be changed, but this date was set in time before the world was created. Please do not think that God can be surprised by our behavior and move the dates of His promise around to fit people's desires. One of the important things to learn as a Believer is that we cannot bargain with God. We must take what He is telling us and make preparations for His return. Jesus told his Disciples that we are not supposed to know the date and day Christ will return (Acts 1:7). I think we can all understand why that date was not given to us. The reason is not to make it a mystery, but to keep us alert and prepared, so the thoughts going through our minds stay focused on serving the Lord everyday of our lives not just the day we think He will return.

Question 2. What will be the Sign of the End of the Age?

Answer: Clarified Verses Below

• **Verses 4 and 5 -** *MANY WILL COME IN MY NAME!*

How many men have come along just in the years we have been on this earth and claimed to be Christ or His equal? Several men come to mind immediately; Hitler, Stalin, Joseph Smith, James Jones, David Koresh, and many others. A variety of men used to come along every few years trying to convince people that they were equal to God. Now, there is a weirdo on every corner of the globe claiming to be God. We see some ministries today that claim that they will be able to be equal to God in the future.

Can we agree that in recent years these things have been ever increasing? Many men have come claiming to be Christ Himself, but their message is usually neutralized because of its content and their character.

Now, let's look at some recent leaders in the church. How many of them have been in trouble with the law? How many of them embezzled millions from their flocks? I know we all make mistakes. Like all of us, even the most spiritual preachers have an evil human nature that constantly battles their spirit. We see men and women of God sin in adultery and come to their flocks for forgiveness. How many of these same people end up going back again and again to the well of forgiveness?

God forgives us without reservation and only He can say when enough is enough. Pastors, elders, deacons, priests, and other spiritual leaders know that they will be held to a higher standard when it comes time to give an account of their lives as shepherds of God's children. The family of God needs to be careful how it picks a spiritual leader. If you hear a lie from your pastor time after time, you may end up believing it yourself. When the time comes for judgment, we will not be able to say, "But Lord, my pastor said it was okay." You are the one who controls how you live for the Lord, not your religious leaders. The Apostle Peter wrote to us about the judgment of God. There will be a punishment that will be very severe for those who do not obey God (1 Peter 4:17).

- **Verse 6 - *You will Hear of Wars and Rumors of Wars. (Don't Be Alarmed)***

Are you aware of how many wars are in progress right this very moment? The United States alone is in a war with several countries that harbor terrorists. Russia is at war with past satellite nations that want to be independent. England has been at war with some of their holdings. Is it reasonable to wonder if Jesus meant these current events of wars and rumors of wars?

The wars among nations, instead of being regional, are now taking on a worldwide aspect. This has been proven by the formation of the United Nations. Each time the United States goes to war, it is with several allies. Soon there will be a one-world government and a one-world army whose enemy will be the church. The church, for the most part, is unaware of just how bad things will be for those who confess Jesus as their Lord.

- **Verse 7- *Nation will rise up against nation. There will be Famines and Earthquakes in Various Places***

Very fewnationsarenotinawarorteeteringonwar.Theconventional definition of war no longer applies. War is as old as mankind itself, but only in the last century have we seen "world" wars, conflicts fought by alliances of many nations against small factions in one or two countries, wars against foes indistinguishable from the civilians they infiltrate, and wars against "terrorism," where the enemy's choice of weapon is usually an unexpected and isolated event, but inflicts extensive and powerful fear. Suicide bombers, computer "hackers," sleeper cells of fanatics just waiting for the right signal, and cultural manipulation of bigotry and discrimination are all modern weapons developed to destroy targeted nations or ways of life. Overshadowing all of this is the danger of nuclear destruction. For many years, only the superpowers had nuclear capability, and the knowledge of mutual retaliation kept them from using it. With the advancement of nuclear technology and its alarming availability to unstable small countries, the prospect of its use is terrifying. Whether it is an extremist walking into an American mall carrying a briefcase containing a tiny nuclear device or a militant country firing a nuclear bomb to "wipe Israel off the map," the risk of global nuclear war is very real and may be looming in the very near future.

Who can remember when there were absolutely no countries described as poverty free? There are so many famines around the world that there is not enough space in this study to name them. There is famine in the United States because of the lack of rain in several areas of this country, while other places close by are flooded. Do you think that perhaps we could say that events like this, when combined with other oddities, could represent an explanation of what is happening during the "Birth Pains" of the "End Times Prophecy?" There were media reports in 2010 saying the number of starving people, the majority of which are children, will surpass that of the previous 100 years. Where water was scarce, we will see more water than we would like. Corn that once was a staple in everyone's diet is now placed on a limited availability because it is grown to be used combined with gasoline to meet emission policies. The New York Times reports that *"Global grain production will tumble by 63 million metric tons in the year of (2011, or 2% over all, mainly because of weather- related calamities like the Russian heat wave and the floods in Pakistan, the United Nations estimates in its most recent report on the world food supply. The United Nations had previously projected that grain yields would grow 1.2 percent this year."* The country of China is now using the majority of rice available worldwide. The United States used to be the main exporter of seasonal produce. China and Brazil have now replaced the U.S.A. A major shift of consumed petroleum and food supplies has taken place without us knowing when it happened. We are quickly becoming a second rate nation. Why is that important to us? The reason is that this country has been blessed beyond description and only because God was the foundation of our land. Now, we have become a nation that rises above God and feels it does not need to hold up God as our Creator. We have become self-sufficient. The problem is we are now feeling the pain of what happens when the hand of God is withdrawn from us. We will never learn, will we?

If we just take a realistic look at our oil production and reserves you will agree we are in serious trouble should another war happen. It should make us all see that we here in the United States are not a privileged society anymore. We never were. God made this country with enough resources to fuel us until His coming, but we allow ignorant men and women to sell our souls to the evil one. We had the blessing of God in all areas of our lives until we concluded that we were in control of our own destiny. The old idea that we were invincible has been proven a myth, and we will see shortly that the power we once held has been reduced to just talk.

- **Verse 8 – *THESE ARE THE BEGINNING OF BIRTH PAINS***

There are so many earthquakes happening around the world, that unless they cost hundreds of lives, we seldom hear about them. This world is becoming desensitized to horrible events and these events are expected to happen on a regular basis. We will soon suffer persecution for our beliefs. And yet this is just the painful time before the real floodgates of persecution begin. If you think it is bad now, just hold on for a little while. We are about to enter a time that most American Christians would never believe we could experience in our lives. Could we say that perhaps we are experiencing "birth pains" in our society that reflect the "birth pains" spoken of in this text? Yes, today the very God we recognize in our constitution is under fire. God has been reduced to mythical status, not the God of creation.

May God have mercy on the souls of those who have taken on the challenge of wiping Him off the map entirely. History does repeat itself. If that is a truism, then we need only read about nations who fought against God and lost. We are in a war we cannot win. Unless we bend our knee toward the Creator of this world, the carnage will be massive.

- **Verse 9a –** *YOU WILL BE PERSECUTED!*

Is Jesus telling us that we here in the United States of America will be suffering persecution because of our beliefs along with millions of Christians around the world? The persecution has already begun in the public arena of this country. No more can we see the Ten Commandments in our public buildings. No more can we see any references to God, unless it is a negative reference. Believers today are ridiculed in the halls of the United States Congress and in our public schools. The name of God is to be spit upon and His name reduced to cartoons. The government gives money to so-called artists who take a picture of the representation of Christ and enclose it in a plastic box of urine. I understand that it is not very pleasant hearing that you will be persecuted for your belief in the Lord, but Jesus has warned you and me of this fact. We will see our belief system challenged by our leaders and our neighbors. If you think that does not affect you, you are very mistaken. This should give you cause to stop and really think about where we are as a world and our relationship with God. Doesn't it sound like these days are upon us and is it time we get serious about our relationship with our Savior?

- **Verse 9b –** *YOU WILL BE HATED AND PUT TO DEATH!*

I have never seen the level of hate in our country that was demonstrated in the elections of 2008 and 2012. That hate has spilled over into the attitudes of many people today. Our culture harbors a huge element of hate. The Islamic nations hate the people of the United States and Christians everywhere. We are quickly becoming a world that will demand one religion. That religion will not be the one that is Biblically based, but will be based on Satan's foundation of evil. Soon chaos will be the order of the day, opening the door for a man to come on the scene as a hero, who turns chaos into calm.

Listen and read what the version of this same event will bring. Mark 13:12, 13…*"Brother will betray brother to death, and a father his child. Children will rebel against their parents and have them put to death. All men will hate you because of me, but he who stands firm to the end will be saved.*

- **Verse 10** – *MANY WILL TURN FROM THE FAITH.*

We have been watching this happen over the past several years. There are numbers being touted by religious leaders claiming that Christianity is growing by leaps and bounds, but these polls are being driven by the selfish desires of man. So called Christians flock to churches that stay away from the warnings of the Bible. Pastors preach feel-good sermons and tell people it is not their fault for being sinners. Your belief system MUST conform to Biblical standards.

A behavior called "situational ethics" has arrived in our mega churches today. The theory is that if you feel it is right, then it is. The church in general today is a church saying to its parishioners that it is God's will that they all be rich and receive the desires of their hearts, without explaining to them the cost of discipleship and the glory of God. A great young preacher studying under the experienced Apostle

Paul listened as Paul explained just how bad things would become in the future world. He told Timothy that people would want to hear only the things that pleased them, and not the sound doctrine they needed. We have reached that prophecy of Paul in our day. (Read 2 Timothy 4:3).

In our time, we see hundreds of thousands of people being put to death because of their religious beliefs. That will soon spread over into North America including the United States, and very soon, the serious persecution of the church will begin. The big question is; are you ready to stand up for the Lord no matter what the circumstances?

- **Verse 11** – *MANY FALSE PROPHETS WILL APPEAR AND DECEIVE MANY PEOPLE*

It is very important that you be able to identify false prophets. You cannot count on someone else to tell you who is, and who is not, a false prophet. That will require that you read the Bible for yourself. Do not take what others, including myself, are saying is the truth. The only way to prove truth is to see if what is being said is backed up by Scripture. If you rely on the Holy Spirit for discernment, He will help you understand. Many false prophets will come from the church. The church has disillusioned them and some have taken the role of false prophets. It is critical that we are aware of what is going on around us to keep from falling into Satan's trap.

We can confirm the subject of my thoughts above by reading the Scripture in the First Book of John as he looks at the subject of antichrists and where they come from. The antichrists John talks about started in the local church (1 John 2:18; 2:22). I am sure that these antichrists heard things that hurt their ears. Jesus expects us to follow His ways, not our own ways. We MUST always listen carefully and discern what is being said to us in church. Please do not misunderstand me. I am not saying be suspicious of your pastor, I am simply saying confirm in the Bible what you are hearing in church. Learn to pay attention to what is being said between the lines of Scripture. Many people think they are not wise enough to glean the message of God in His Book. Do not believe that lie! God does have a plan for your life and you will be pleasantly surprised at what He has in store for you.

The first thing all people should do is to determine where their relationship with Christ stands. Is He just someone you have heard about in church or by others, but you have not accepted Him as your Savior? Christ wants to have a personal relationship with you. It is His desire that you prove all things by reading His words in the Bible.

- **Verses 12-13 - _STAND FIRM TO THE END_**

Related Verse / Habakkuk 2:3...*For the revelation awaits an appointed time; it speaks of the end <u>and will not prove false</u>. Though it linger, wait for it; <u>it will certainly come</u> and will not delay.*

This is a message to the church about church members. The church will be on the receiving end of wickedness. Many will not be able to withstand the pressures of this time. This is an early warning system given to us by our Savior. Many people lose their lives because they do not heed this early warning system. Do not let this happen to you. Jesus said that these things will happen and you can be sure that they will. You may think that those going through the Tribulation will be unjustly persecuted. However, Jesus has given these Believers a special time with Him as He allows them to rule with Him on the transformed earth for 1000 years.

If you are a "Pew Sitter" in church and never crack open your Bible, either at church or in your home, YOU WILL NOT HAVE WHAT

IT TAKES TO STAND FIRM IN CHRIST. I am not trying to be hurtful or challenge your Salvation, but what I am saying is that Jesus expects more from you than keeping a pew warm on Sunday morning. Please read James 1:2-24.

- **Verse 14 -** *The Gospel Preached Worldwide*

Everyone will hear the Gospel message before Jesus will come. There will be no one who will be able to say to the Lord on that Day of Judgment that he or she did not hear about Christ. The time for excuses is over. If your name is not written in the Book of Life, then your next home will be in the Lake of Burning Sulfur forever. Now you have an option to accept Jesus or reject Him. Be very careful how you choose; your eternal life is at stake.

Take a moment to read again the words in Revelation 14:6 that explain how the last warning of the Gospel is given to man. *"Then I saw another angel flying in midair, and he had the <u>eternal gospel</u> to proclaim to those who live on the earth--to <u>every nation</u>, tribe, language and people. He said in a loud voice, "<u>Fear God and give him glory</u>, because the hour of his judgment has come. <u>Worship him</u> who made the heavens, the earth, the sea and the springs of water."* No one will be able to say that they were not told about the Gospel of Christ.

Many people do not know the Gospel of Christ, and will not follow the commands of Jesus because they have ignored or rejected Him. Who fears God these days, no matter how huge the disaster? Oh, yes, after the events of September 2001 people packed the churches for about two weeks. Once the shock of the event calmed down, God once again took last place in the lives of many Americans. Who will worship Him and give Him the glory He deserves? Worshipping God has become something that is looked upon as a weakness in an individual. People will cover their ears when anyone begins to tell them of a man called Jesus.

Jesus continues with what we are to be looking for in those last days. The following is a warning of impending doom. The word of God will be perverted as never before. Luke 21:16-18, *"You will be betrayed even by parents, brothers, relatives and friends, and they will put some of you to death. All men will hate you because of me. But not a hair of your head will perish."*

• **Verse 15 - _THE ABOMINATION - CAUSES DESOLATION_**

Just who, or what, is the abomination that causes desolation? The abomination is a living statue of the antichrist that will be constructed in a wing of the Temple. As the Tribulation begins, the antichrist will make a treaty between the Arab Nations and Israel. For the first three and a half years, peace will be the message of the antichrist. That message will be accepted by the nations of the world (Daniel 9:27).

The Jews will be able to worship by bringing sacrifices to the Temple. My guess is (and this is pure speculation) that the Muslim Palestinians will give up the "Dome of the Rock" for a land of their own, so the Jews can rebuild their own Temple on the Holy Site where it originally once stood.

However, for the sake of peace and a trade for land, it is possible that such a deal could be made. During the peace segment of the Tribulation, the antichrist will have a wing of the Temple in which he will be working on the construction of an image of himself. The abomination is an idol of a false god (the antichrist) that will desecrate the Temple and the name of God. This event will be worse than spilling pig's blood over the floors of the Temple of our Holy Father.

This is also confirmation that the Jews will be given their site back for the Temple of God. It will sit on the site that right this moment has the symbol of the Islamic Nation, the Dome of the Rock. You would be hard pressed to find any Muslim who would say that one day the Temple of God would be rebuilt on the Rock. That shows just how charismatic the antichrist will be, even to the Muslim world. With all the wondrous things done by the antichrist, who will not be deceived by him? Only those who have read and understood what Jesus said would happen in The End will endure.

There is a view that Believers will not be able to be deceived by the antichrist. It is very dangerous to assume the verses in Matthew Chapter 24:24-25 mean that the church will be protected from being deceived. There is protection of the Believers, but it will be through the knowledge of what Jesus is telling them throughout the Book of Revelation and the seal that has been put on their heads. Strength to overcome the antichrist comes from the Holy Spirit within them, and by Christ fulfilling His promise to cut short the persecution of the saints.

Once again, the power of the antichrist will be so strong that, although it would appear that Believers could not be tricked, they can and will be. We must remember that there is only one Christ and He will return exactly how He says in His Revelation.

Much of the book of Daniel addresses the "End Time" concerning gathering of the church. He explains what the antichrist will do and how he will deceive many of those who are Believers. Daniel tells us that the antichrist will broker a peace settlement with many people, especially the nation of Israel (Daniel 9:27). Notice Daniel did not say this agreement would be with all people. Many Christians will recognize who he is and will begin to go into a Tribulation mode, for which they have been getting ready for, for many years. It is so important that the church takes the time to know the Book of Revelation and to understand the horrible mistake of being caught off guard, thus losing their security of a new home for eternity in heaven with Christ. Remember please, your security in Christ is your responsibility (1 John 2:18-27).

- **Verses 16,17,18,19 – *GET OUT OF JUDEA!***

The four verses here tell us that danger is coming. If you are a Jew or a Believer of the Christ of God, it will be time to head for the hills. In other words, get as far away from the cities as you can. We know that persecution will be coming for those who belong to Christ.

The main target as this persecution begins, will be those people who belong to Jesus. The authorities will demand that they denounce Christ. Can you imagine the dread of pregnant women and nursing mothers? As they flee the cities, Christian women will be forced to give birth in the back seats of cars, in dark filthy alleys, or any place they can find to deliver their babies safely and without detection. They will be in constant fear of being betrayed to the authorities by people trying to gain favor with the government, including families, friends, and neighbors. Nursing mothers must have adequate water and nutrition. Women with young infants will not only have to keep their babies safe and healthy; they will need to keep them quiet. Many have heard of the young Jewish mother who accidentally smothered her baby to death trying to keep the Nazis from hearing its cry and discovering the family hiding in the basement. Some think this verse is merely symbolic, but all

Believers must safeguard these women as their struggles are intensified by their flight from danger.

- **Verse 20 - *WINTER SEASON AND SABBATH***

The horror of the situation will be indescribable for those remaining Believers when the False Prophet reveals the antichrist for who he really is. As we approach Mid-Tribulation, the pressure brought to bear on the Christian community will be horrible. Believers will have to hide from a central government. This new government will be determined to kill all those who believe in God and His Son Jesus. Many of these killings will be in the form of beheading. Children will be held as ransom until their parents denounce Jesus. Once they do that, their eternal life will be spent in the Lake of Burning Sulfur. The children will be with Christ because of their age, assuming the children have not reached the age of accountability.

When we add the perils of winter to this mix, we can understand why Christ would ask us to pray about the season of Judgments and His return. Those who experience the Birth Pains will be stunned as they see the persecution targeted toward them as Believers.

The Sabbath day was made to be a Holy Day for man. If all of this torment was finalized on the last days before the return of Christ in the clouds with His angels, how ironic it would be if death and destruction were the order of the day for the day called the Sabbath. How important will it be to recognize that long ago our Lord warned us of these coming events? How absolutely sad it will be if we are so puffed up that we thought we would escape the last days; especially since Jesus spent twenty two chapters in the book of Revelation telling exactly what will happen. If you have elected to ignore His pleas to accept Him as your Savior, it is unlikely that you will do so in these circumstances either. I plead with you to read what God has for you in the Word of God, the Bible.

- **Verses 21, 22 – *THE DIFFERENCE OF THE JUDGMENTS OF CHRIST AND THE WRATH OF GOD***

The distress the world will experience will be greater than anyone's imagination and will never be equaled again! Now, I want to make sure you understand this next verse. It says: *"If those days* [of great distress] *had not been cut short, no one would survive, but for the sake of the elect those days will be shortened.* This does not say that the elect will not experience those days of distress, but it does say that the days will be shortened <u>because</u> of the elect. Be careful of antichrists who say you are so special that you will be spared persecution for the name of Christ. Why have many Christians been persecuted and had their heads cut off for Christ through today? Why were they not taken off this earth before they had to suffer? Consider those hundreds of thousands of Christians in Africa who were beheaded for the Lord in just the last few years. This atrocity happened in the nation of Sudan and other neighboring countries in 2009-2011.

- **Verse 23 –** *WE REPLACE GOD WITH SELF AND OTHER FALSE PROPHETS*

Let's just take one moment to speak of what is happening in the United States. What have we done to God who gave us such a wonderful country? When the pilgrims left England to come to this country, it was like the Jews crossing the Jordan River into the land of milk and honey. Was the wish of our forefathers that we abandon the God for whom they sacrificed and died? Our answer is a resounding NO! Yet now we are allowing our country to grow distant from the God who gave us such a wonderful nation. What is happening to our country as we stand by and watch evil people destroy what our forefathers worked so hard to establish? What will our story look like in just a few short years? I suggest, unless we step up and put God back on His Throne, we too will become a homeless people who will be looked at as less than human.

Although we see this happening, we seem to be in a mindset of retreat within ourselves and to be content with our situation. We can see young and old people getting weary of their circumstances in life, and are watching them hit the streets looking for others to give them help. We stand by and watch this country turn to the socialistic atrocity that is failing miserably in Europe, the same system our forefathers sacrificed to get away from. It is difficult to stand by and watch as citizens of this country protest the free society that God has blessed us with, and we stand by watching as if there will be no effect. Those who wish to be taken care of by the government will live to see the day when they will regret losing what their parents and grandparents experienced as they lived in a free country.

- **Verse 24 - *Millions Turn from the Lord Their Grandparents Once Knew***

False prophets will appear performing miracles to deceive the elect. The last few words of this verse about deceiving the elect (if that were possible) do not mean that it is impossible to deceive the elect. As we read in verse 10, *"many will turn away from the faith."* People can try to spin this in any way they want, but the facts are listed here concerning signs of the end of the age. It is crystal clear that the church will be here to experience some of the atrocities brought about by the rebellion of the human race and Satan. Please, do not be led astray by false doctrine. We will not be able to blame others for our mistakes when choosing who we follow into eternity.

Question 3. *What will be the Sign of His Coming?*

The answer to this question is found in Matthew, Chapter 24:29-31. Jesus speaks here of those Christians who have followed Him and obeyed His commands. He explains that He will send His angels to collect those who believed in Him and accepted Him as their Savior. The entire world will hear this event, and will witness the gathering of the Saints of Christ by His angels. This will be verified as we read later in Chapter Eleven of Revelation about the Harvesting of His Believers before the Wrath of God will be poured out on those who have received the Mark of the Beast and rejected God's Son as their Savior. There is no question that ALL of the earth will see Him.

Then Jesus goes on to tell what will happen after He comes in the clouds to take His church out of a rapidly imploding earth because of its negative behavior toward God and His Son.

1. The sun will be darkened
2. The moon will not give light
3. The stars will fall from the sky

We will discuss these three things in detail when we start the actual study of the Book of Revelation in our next segment. Please understand that there IS NOT a Third Coming of Christ! Jesus talks only of one more return to this world. Revelation Chapter 14 tells us about the Harvesting of the elect by the angels. This account in Revelation is in concert with Matthew 24:31. Jesus will return to this old earth just one more time, and that will be His Second Coming. If Jesus were to come to earth to earth any sooner, He would be unusually inconsistent in His teachings. There are several theories that we will investigate as we go along in the book of Revelation. You are probably more familiar with what is called a Pre-Tribulation Rapture theory. Some of you may have been taught a Mid-Tribulation Rapture theory. You will come to a conclusion for yourself as we look at the message that Jesus left us describing when He will come for His church, and when He will come the last time with great power and judgment.

Once we begin to look at this when studying the Revelation of Jesus the Christ, we will see that the book of Revelation is not written in chronological order. Certain things are mentioned and then put into sequence by future writings. All of this will be explained as we get into the book itself.

Christ had just previously told the disciples about the torment of the Tribulation period. His concern is that we would not be found sleeping and thus miss the reward of His coming. Be on guard! Be alert! This was the warning of Christ for His church. Other accounts of His coming can be found in Mark Chapter 13 and Luke Chapter 21.

Matthew 24:44 instructs us to always be ready for His return. To be ready we must be able to recognize the signs of the return of Christ. We must be careful of otherwise well-meaning men and women who tell us that Jesus is returning early so the church can be spared the persecution described by Jesus throughout the New Testament and His prophets in times past. We will look at some of the older writings of Scripture to verify all that I am saying in this book.

Several people, including well-known evangelists and preachers, have predicted the Second Coming of Christ. Some have continued to set the date of Christ's return even after being wrong time after time. It is very important that we do not cause confusion within the church concerning the return of Christ. If Christ were to return to this earth for His church and then return after the Wrath of God with His Saints, it would not be called the Second Coming of Christ, it would be called The Third Coming of Christ. To clear up any confusion, His angels gather (harvest) the saints up to meet Jesus in the clouds just before the final Wrath of God.

Wouldn't it have been easier for us if God the Father had shared the exact date that His Son was returning for His church? Of course not! We would lose the reverent fear of God that we need to continue in His ways. We would lose our sense of urgency to share the Gospel of Christ with the world. We would not keep Christ as the priority in our life that is needed to walk in the path He has laid out for us. It is safe to say that there would not be many churches built to worship God and honor the Savior. We have people today who say, "I will accept Christ as my Savior, later." Can you imagine the excuses that would be expressed if we knew the date of His coming? People around the world would feel that this date was a fraud and pay no attention it, to their own demise.

So what God did, in His wisdom, was to share with us some signs that we would be able to see that would indicate when The End time was drawing near. These signs would be something we could see and experience, which would be an indicator that His Son's coming was nearing. These events should not only be a reminder that we need to "clean up our act", but that we should increase our passion to share the Blessed Hope with others. We have to be prepared every single day, because we have no idea when God will require our life. If we are to overcome the world until the return of Christ Jesus, we have to stand firm in our faith until the end, and the only way to accomplish that is to stay rooted in the Bible on a daily basis.

I should point out here that multiple generations before our time have predicted that they would be the one that marked the coming of Christ. Even the early churches felt that Christ would return at anytime. There were wars and rumors of wars. There were pestilences and earthquakes from time to time. There were even antichrists that popped up occasionally. I remember that when this country was in the "Cold War" with the Soviet Union, we thought for sure Christ would be coming soon. The problem is that we have become desensitized about the return of Christ for His church. Instead of reading what Jesus requires of us as His disciples in the last days, we seem to want to focus on His return, preferably before the Tribulation so we can forgo any persecution personally. Men and women have been persecuted for Christ since the days when He came to earth to give us hope for the future. We read about the desensitizing of the people in I Thessalonians 5:1-3, where Paul tells how the coming of the Lord will come as a shock to the people of this world. They will not be expecting Him.

In this age, we can see the bigger picture because of instant and expansive television coverage. We see the Middle East in turmoil like never before, and the chances for peace in that area diminish daily. There is never a shortage of peace plans being presented to the people in the area, but none of these peace proposals have worked.

There is a man coming on the scene soon who will offer a plan to Israel that will be acceptable and for a few years things will look much better than before.

We have seen many peace treaties come along between Israel and other nations surrounding it. None of these treaties have held. The Bible suggests that conditions will be right for all Arab nations to sign a peace treaty with Israel. Right now, we are seeing a heavy handed, strong movement toward a so-called democracy in the Middle East. What this phony democracy will accomplish is to draw all of the Arab nations closer and, as one, they will follow the antichrist.

We know what the world will be doing when He does come. Right up to the very moment when Christ returns, people will be oblivious to His coming. I do not write this to be redundant, but I want to impress on you the seriousness of these days during the Tribulation period. Matthew 24: 37-39 tells us that the world will be *as it was in the days of Noah.*" Noah's story matches up well with what is going on in our world today. Can you hear the laughter as Noah tells people about the amount of water that is coming their way? They had no idea what rain was since all of their gardens were watered from the internal water in the earth. We will be without excuse when Jesus comes just as the people were in Noah's time. The penalty will be just as final in that there will be little chance to accept God's Son as He offers Salvation right up until His church is harvested after the last trumpet sounds. All of this information may be difficult to understand, even to the point of accepting it as the truth; yet God's word stands as truth (Rev. 1:16-19).

Peter gives us another look at the end times in 2 Peter 3:3-7. He begins by telling us about what our ears are hearing right at this moment in time. People are indeed scoffing at Christian and Jewish principles concerning the idea that men will live beyond what they know as a worldly life. Peter reminds the people that long ago Jesus created the world out of water, and that same water destroyed the entire human race, with the exception of Noah and his family. We, as the human race today, should wake up and realize what a terrible situation we have created for ourselves.

What do we see today? Is there anything happening in our time that would cause you to believe that the end is near? God is being shoved into a closet designed by Satan himself. He knows that the more he can convince people to abandon their basic feelings that there is a God, the less they will attempt to find Him. When we look back to the excitement of our forefathers landing on the shores of this country and now see what we have allowed it to become, we should tremble before God. There is a time coming when all of us will have to give an account to God for our lives while here on earth. May God have mercy on our souls!

Now, it is not my desire to get everybody depressed as we see what our future looks like. However, it is my intention to tell you the truth of the events that God has foretold us concerning the End Times, including the preparation we need to make as we see the signs of the end. When you have completed this study, you will not be standing back wringing your hands, but you will finally feel a sense of security that most Christians have never felt.

The account written plainly by the Savior was believed by the nations from the time of His ministry until the early nineteenth century. Then came another account of the coming of Christ conjured up by a little teenage girl in Scotland that dishonest men changed into a lie. Several ministers actually fought over who came up with this theory first. Well-meaning men and women have taught this heresy from 1830 until this very day. They were forced to do this because they would lose thousands of dollars and their jobs if the congregations were told the truth. Woe to anyone misrepresenting the Coming of Christ that will cause "The Great Falling Away".

Foundational Chapters

BETWEEN THE CHAPTERS

Words and Meanings

Surely, the Sovereign Lord does nothing without revealing His plan to His servants the prophets (Amos 3:7).

- **Revelation** / Divine spiritual disclosure revealing events predestined to occur.
  Habakkuk 2:3...*For the revelation awaits an appointed time; it speaks of the end and will not prove false. Though it linger, wait for it; it will certainly come and will not delay.*

- **Blessed...Blessing** / This word speaks directly to the passing down of the power of the Throne Room of God to all who will accept that Jesus is the Christ of God.
  *Malachi 2:2...If you do not listen, and if you do not resolve to honor my name," says the LORD Almighty, "I will send a curse on you, and I will curse your **blessings**. Yes, I havealready cursed them, because you have not resolved to honor me.*

- **Apocalyptic** / The book of Revelation discloses the "End Times" by stripping back conjecture and forecasts the true meaning about the end of this world, which includes the events of the "Harvesting of the Saints" along with the "Second Coming of the Christ."

- **Angelic interaction** / Angels play a huge part in End Times and the Revelation of Christ. We will read of "Mighty Angels" and "Special Angels." Jesus will use thousands of angels from the Throne Room of God to tell His story.

- **ETERNITY** / *The dictionary defines eternity as an "infinite or unending time," or an "endless life after death."*

CHAPTER 1

The Two Blessings of Christ

Read – Chapter 1:1-2

What you are about to read will, at times, take your breath away. John will soon find himself in the presence of those in the Throne Room of God. We all should put ourselves in John's shoes as he is beginning to get personally re-acquainted with the Christ of God whom he had earlier seen die on the cross and then be raised from the tomb by God. John heard the words of Jesus just before He was taken up to heaven in the clouds. His feelings must have run the gamut from wonder and awe to awesome terror. Even though this was the John who was known as "the Disciple whom Jesus loved," their earlier relationship did little to calm the anxiety of the Apostle.

John always had a good relationship with Christ during His ministry. We must remember that Jesus had received the glory of God when He was raised from the grave, so the sight of the Son of God had to be overwhelming even though Jesus had talked often to the disciples about the future, especially when He described His Father in heaven (John 21:20).

As you have just read in the first two verses of Revelation, God was going to give John the Revelation of Christ Jesus. John would then be responsible for recording all that would be shown to him. God will begin this prophecy of the future by sending His angel to John and explaining all that would be shown to him. The angel used the word <u>MUST</u> when referring to what would be happening soon to this world. You may be a little confused about the words "very soon." How long is the word "soon" as we use it in a sentence? I will return soon was the promise of a famous general in World War II. "Soon" turned out to be longer than anyone expected. I will not attempt to establish any return date of Christ based on these verses and neither should you. We must always trust only Scripture to confirm prophecies about the timing of God.

Related Verses: */ 2 Peter 3:8-9…But do not forget this one thing, dear friends: With the Lord a day is like a thousand years, and a thousand years are like a day. The Lord is not slow in keeping his promise, as some understand slowness. He is patient with you, not wanting anyone to perish, but everyone to come to repentance.*

Peter reminds us that a day is like a thousand years to God. Although God created the earth in seven real twenty-four hour days, in the case of working toward the end of the earth, there is no timing but God's timing. If indeed a day to God is like 1000 years, then surely we can understand that time is in His hands and we need to concentrate on what our position is in the family of God and what we should be doing with the time He has given us. Our responsibility is to be sharing the Gospel with others and being ready to leave this earth and be with our Lord at His timing. It is not an accident that you are here at this juncture of world events. Pay careful attention to the gifts God has given you and work hard to use those gifts for Him.

Although we will look back on many references in the Old and New Testaments, our study will concentrate mainly on what Jesus said would happen as the time draws near to what is defined as the "End Time" of this world as told through the Revelation that Christ has given us. Jesus confirms much of the text written about His return in both the New and Old Testaments. Although other passages throughout the Bible refer to the "End Times" if the book of Revelation was all we had to explain this event, it would stand alone in explaining all that will happen.

Please remember that Christ said that He came for those who needed Him, and that the wise would reject Him. We see that happening when the so-called wise men of our age have changed the book of truth into a book of fables. They have taken verses from the various books of the Bible and tried to put them together as if it were a jigsaw puzzle. What we do here is combine other passages outside of the Book of Revelation, but in the Bible, to fit together as if this were a group of gears all working together. We will cover many verses of the Bible that are briefly recorded in Matthew 24; Mark 13; John 16; Luke 17; and Luke 21 among many other supporting passages.

Let me say here once again, that what we are reading in the book of Revelation will be the complete chronicle of the Harvesting of the Saints and the Second Coming of Christ. While it is true that we can use the Old Testament to verify much of what I will be saying in this book, there is no one more qualified to tell us of the End Time events than Christ Himself. Everything that a Born-Again family member of God needs to know about when Jesus is coming again is written in this book of the Canon. Let me offer a word of caution to those who would like to add or take away the message that Jesus so carefully made available for us. We will be very clear about the messages given to us in the book of Revelation when explaining how Christ will redeem His family (Harvest), and His Second Coming. Any other theories of the return of Christ to this world cannot use the book of Revelation for resource material. Oh yes, many have tried to distort the message of Christ and have been very successful. I ask you to please listen to the Holy Spirit as you read these verses. He will never deceive you and He will give you a peace that will confirm you have read the text correctly.

John will be telling us of things he saw personally. However, there will be some things that he was asked not to record. We will know about those mysteries someday in the timing of Jesus. It has always been the custom of Jewish law that there had to be at least two witnesses to confirm an event. In the Revelation of the things to come in this world, Jesus went one step further. John was a witness to what was forthcoming along with Christ, who was showing him what would happen, and then the final witness is God the Father. We can take what is written here in this book to be the truth that will stand alone with the facts. Oh yes, there will be a lot of other Scriptures in both the Old and the New Testaments that verify these events, but if all we had was this book of Revelation, we would know what is ahead. As we read in John 8:18, these two witnesses are solid and can be relied on for the truth. In a world of deception, it is a wonderful feeling knowing we can turn to God for truth.

Daniel 2:27-28 speaks to the issue of God revealing the truth, and God is the only one who can reveal future events based on His words alone. Since God is the author of truth, we do not question His Revelation to us. We either have faith that what He says is true, or we insert man's wisdom or twist the Scriptures to fit our comfort zone.

Parents have an obligation to pass down to their children the blessing or promise of love before they enter society without us by their side. They need to feel our blessings, taking them one step closer to a productive life with confidence of our faith in their abilities. Jesus promises us words of blessing by passing down to us a confident message of hope, peace, and comfort in the most difficult time of trouble.

Jesus starts off His message with blessings, but will also end His prophecy to us by pointing out that we MUST make a decision concerning where we will spend our eternal life.

Read – Chapter 1:3

Here we read about two blessings that are ours to receive just for following what the Lord is asking of us. The first blessing given to us is for reading this book of prophecy. The blessing God is giving us for such a small request is His knowledge that will take away the doubt and fear in our life in the End Times. If we follow the teaching of Christ, we can count on a life, although scattered with mountains to climb, filled with His indescribable peace in times of extreme turmoil.

Just for reading the book of Revelation, you and I receive a blessing from the Throne Room of God. Included in this blessing will be that as End Time events begin to happen, you will be aware of what is going on and take appropriate action. It also means that you will pass down through the generations what the truth of the Harvesting of the Saints and the Second Coming of Christ will look like. You and I may not see the Great Tribulation, but it could mean that your children or grandchildren may indeed see Christ as they are lifted up to Him in the clouds (1 Thess. Chapter 4:16-17).

The subject of the passing down of the End Time events is so important that many verses of Scripture have been written telling us to make sure our children are taught the past and the future correctly. Psalm 78:5-6 tells us of Jacob being told a new law in Israel that fathers were to teach their children about the events of the past.

This was important for the well being of the future generations. Now today, we should be telling the truth to our children so they will be able to foresee the future that will bring about persecution that they could never have imagined.

This is extremely important because millions of Christians have been duped by well meaning Christian leaders. However, the result of their deception will lead to millions of people renouncing their relationship with Christ. Even the leaders will be shocked when they must give an account for their lives.

Prophecy should not be given by those who can be caught up in the theories of men that have been created by twisting the Scriptures to give a theory that is untrue. All prophecy has to be a result of the Holy Spirit speaking to men and women concerning the truth of the Scriptures. There are no different theories concerning the Tribulation or any other subject that has not been clearly defined in the words of God in the Holy Bible. Of course, we can take out words and add words, which will completely change the message. That is why the Apostle James wrote to us in his epistle that not many of us should make the decision on our own to be teachers of the Word of God. Teachers of the Scriptures will be held to a higher standard (James 3:1).

Most men and women accept what they are taught by their religious leaders. Many pastors may feel threatened by parishioners who take the time after the service to go home and verify what they were told in a church setting. Prophecy coming from the pulpit should always be verified by Biblical facts through the Scriptures. Most parents understand what they are hearing in church will be passed down through the centuries by their children and grandchildren. If what we teach them is wrong, we are the ones who will be responsible for not researching and verifying what we are being told is accurate and indeed the Word of God. However, our students or parishioners must hold our feet to the fire by reading the Scripture, thus proving to them that spiritual matters taught to them are true.

The second blessing that we receive from these early verses in Revelation is one that requires us to take action. We must take what has been written as truth and apply it to our lives. Christ tells us why this is so important when speaking of the End Time. In fact, He uses the words "take to heart" to believe what He is saying and what is written in the book of Revelation (Revelation 1:3; Matthew 9:2; 9:22).

It is important to understand a couple of things when speaking about the end of this world. First, there is an End Time when the world as we know it will cease to exist. Secondly, there is also a time when we will come to the end of <u>our own life</u> in this world. It is great to understand what Jesus is saying about His Second Coming, and how we will see Him when we leave this earth, either by death or by a time of harvesting His family.

However, billions have passed from life to death long before the promised return of Christ. What does that mean for us? It means that we MUST pick with whom we would like to spend eternity. We have that choice while we are still living. That choice is either to accept Jesus and be "Born Again," or reject Him and select eternity in the Lake of Burning Sulfur with Satan. So accept these two blessings and live for the Lord. He has a life for you and awaits your decision.

Read – Chapter 1:4-8

Verse four begins the letter to the seven churches of Asia. These churches were in somewhat of a circle that was close to the heart of Asia. These churches also were an example of the unity of the membership even though they were in distinctly different social settings. I believe these Scripture, thus proving to them that spiritual matters taught to them are true.

The second blessing that we receive from these early verses in Revelation is one that requires us to take action. We must take what has been written as truth and apply it to our lives. Christ tells us why this is so important when speaking of the End Time. In fact, He uses the words "take to heart" to believe what He is saying and what is written in the book of Revelation (Revelation 1:3; Matthew 9:2; 9:22).

It is essential to understand a couple of things when speaking about the end of this world. First, there is an End Time when the world as we know it will cease to exist. Secondly, there is also a time when we will come to the end of <u>our own life</u> in this world. It is great to understand what Jesus is saying about His Second Coming, and how we will see Him when we leave this earth, either by death or by a time of harvesting His family.

However, billions have passed from life to death long before the promised return of Christ. What does that mean for us? It means that we MUST pick with whom we would like to spend eternity. We have that choice while we are still living. That choice is either to accept Jesus and be "Born Again," or reject Him and select eternity in the Lake of Burning Sulfur with Satan. So accept these two blessings and live for the Lord. He has a life for you and awaits your decision.

Read – Chapter 1:4-8

Verse four begins the letter to the seven churches of Asia. These churches were in somewhat of a circle that was close to the heart of Asia. These churches also were an example of the unity of the membership even though they were in distinctly different social settings. I believe these churches were selected by Christ for us to examine how we should conduct ourselves today. Each of these churches had unique problems and shared some positive attributes. The bottom line to all of them was whatever their problems were that prevented them from enjoying a perfect relationship with Christ, they were to wake up and change their ways.

John uses a typical greeting for those Christians in that period in history. He says, "Grace and Peace" to you. This greeting is directly from Christ Jesus to not only these churches, but to all of us even today. The words "grace" and "peace." represent the core values of the relationship in the family of God. This greeting also tells us just who Christ is and where He comes from. Mark speaks of eternity, both past and future, which includes Christ's future return in the clouds for His followers as the final sacrifice (Mark 13:26).

Jesus was there in eternity past and will always be there for us in the eternal future. Jesus was sent to us by the "I AM." That is Father God. The relationship between the Son of God and the LORD would forever be changed when Jesus became obedient to His Father even to the point of death on the cross. He thereafter would be called the Son of the living God. Many people have a hard time processing just who

God is and who Jesus is. Read the verse below to help those having trouble. Exodus 3:14, 15 explains just who God is. God says that, "I AM WHO I AM." Since all of the attributes of God are incorporated in His Son Jesus; Christ must hold the same power and authority as His Father. To understand who Christ is means that all we need do is look at His Father. They are as one, even when being separated when Jesus came to earth and God was in heaven. Jesus said nothing on His own initiative, but He spoke the thoughts and words of His Father, God (John 5:30; John 8:54).

Not all people accept the idea of eternity for a man's soul as something that is possible. I will admit that wrapping our minds around the thought of living forever is a hard thing to do. However, we must be ready to live the eternal life that we choose. It can be in the Paradise of God in a New Heaven and a New Earth, or it can be in the Lake of Burning Sulfur. Now to me, that is an easy choice, but many people will not make a selection and end up in hell by default. No matter who the skeptic is, deep in his heart is a nagging thought about life after death here on earth. The soul of man will not let him live without a small voice calling him to believe. Without getting into a lengthy conversation about the eternity of man, let's just say that you believe you have a soul from God and that soul is eternal, or you don't. Understanding the book of Revelation brings with it an assumption that the person reading the verses is reading with an open heart and is aware of the guidance of the Holy Spirit. That being the case, everything you will need to know about the "end time" of this world is written in the Bible. God has made it abundantly clear to man about who He is and how He made this world. When you doubt this, you do it at your own peril.

Of course, we can read prophecy concerning these times, and many passages in the New Testament referring to the Harvesting of the Saints, and Second Coming of Christ. Revelation is not a book in which we can read the words one time and walk away knowing all there is to know about the Second Coming of Christ, let alone the time of the Harvesting of the Saints.

The critical thing to learn here is that we all, including you and me, will have to give an account for our lives no matter when we die. If we die prior to the Tribulation Period, we will go to a place and await our time to give an account of our life. Those places we go to until the

Harvesting of the Saints or the Second Coming of Christ, are either Hades or the Paradise of God. There is a huge difference in the living conditions between Hades and Paradise.

I will spend little time here speaking of what Paradise is like, but I want to say some words about Hades. I believe there is evidence from the Scriptures that Hades is like a place in the deepest part of this earth. At this very moment it has a population of fallen angels who are awaiting judgment along with those who turned their back on God and those who rejected Jesus as the Savior of the world. I can tell you that there is an entrance to this place here on earth where an iron gate is covering the hole into which Satan will be thrown one day. Hades is the place where evil has its source (2 Peter 2:4; Revelation 20:1).

There are verses in Revelation 20:12-15 that speak of a time when we all will give an account for our life while here on earth. When we consider the only two places we will spend eternity, it is wise to look at our lives and take a spiritual inventory of what our life will look like while standing in front of our Creator. This should be food for thought and let all remember that there will be no excuses.

In verse five, Jesus explains more about who He is and what His position is in relationship to the world and its inhabitants. Jesus had just explained there were "seven spirits" before the throne, which represented the "seven churches" which He would soon address. Jesus is the first to be brought up out of the grave alive, after His death by crucifixion before many witnesses. Jesus is the first man to die, and then be brought back to life to live eternally. Victory over death was His. God demonstrated to the world that Jesus is the King of all Kings of the earth and that He has defeated death. This victory over death was passed down to all of us who would accept Jesus as our Savior. The body we have now will die, but our soul will immediately be alive in a new eternal body without defect in the Paradise of God. In Paradise, we will wait for a glorified body when Christ brings all of His family together in heaven as described in Revelation 11:15-19. Jesus speaks of those under the altar of God as they receive white robes while they wait for their fellow saints who will join them shortly. We will talk more about these souls under the altar in Chapter Six.

Those under the altar of God will lose their earthly lives by being beheaded during the Tribulation. We must remember that the degree of persecution will be intense during the "time of trouble." Still, the love of the Father will be with us as we continue to serve Him no matter the trouble.

John explains that God loved us so much that He sent Jesus to live the life of a man; and then die for the sins of all men; and then to seal the relationship as Jesus' blood was offered to cleanse the sin of Adam, and all other transgressions. The love of Christ knows no bounds. He loves the entire world. Unfortunately, the only people who will experience His love will be those who love Him. Jesus then tells us of the glory of His Father God whom we serve (John 3:16).

In verse seven, John begins by telling us what the return of Christ will look like. Because this verse shows us what will happen at the end of the world, it would seem that this verse would be better placed near the end of the book of Revelation. God placed it here to impress on all those who read it that He is God and we MUST listen to what He is warning us about as the End Time nears. Please notice what the angel said to John, "*every eye will see Him.*" That should be great comfort for John and for us. Those who beat and scourged Jesus need to see Him as the Lord of Lords, and the One who will judge their sins.

The next sentence should shake the world. He said, "*The earth will mourn because of Him.*" Not only would men mourn for Him because of the atrocities He had to endure to assure man eternal life with Him: they would mourn because they elected to reject the love Jesus offered them. They traded eternal life in the Paradise of God for a few years on this earth without accountability and an eternity in hell.

Once again, we will look at the Book of Daniel the prophet. In one of his spiritual moments, Daniel saw Jesus coming on the clouds. Notice in these verses he did not say coming to earth, he said coming on the clouds! Daniel was brought before Christ in this vision to show him the absolute authority Jesus would have over man. There is no corner of the earth where Christ will not be worshiped and identified as One whose kingdom will never pass away. His kingdom was so strong that it would never be destroyed by any power in this world or any world to come (Daniel 7:13-14). Once again in Revelation 1:8, Jesus said that He was here in the beginning and will be here forever. This verse leaves no question about who Jesus is and the authority He has over His creation. He says that He is the beginning and the end, "who was, and is to come." This is affirmed repeatedly in Revelation (1:8; 21:6; 22:13).

Read – Chapter 1:9-11

These verses begin the story of what John sees and hears over the next few days. John immediately identifies himself as one among many who were being persecuted for the kingdom of God. Like others, John found himself on the island of Patmos for the cause of Christ. Patmos was one of many islands that were used by the Romans to exile men and women who were radical political people and considered religious zealots that caused uprisings among the population. The preaching of the Gospel back then was just as unpopular as it is today. John had many idle hours to spend with Jesus in meditation and prayer. I say that, but I want you to know that John's time on this island was not like a vacation. Although none of us can tell what it was like on this island, we can speculate that being a prisoner of the Roman government was terrible.

Many men and women find Jesus when sentenced to prison or jail. Once one has reached the bottom of the social scale, the only place to look is upward. It is not unusual for them to study many hours each day. This time results in growth very quickly in the knowledge of the word of God. In the case of John, I can see him being an outspoken Apostle of Christ Jesus and I would presume many prisoners came to know the love of God as they heard about the death of Jesus on the cross for their sins. Many may want to put a modernistic spin on what is called the Lord's Day in this passage. The Lord's Day here was no doubt on a Saturday. It is not very critical other than to point out that this was a special day. When you are incarcerated, everyday can be the Lord's Day. I believe that John still observed Saturday as the Sabbath. Unfortunately, it is very difficult to get people to recognize God on any day of the week. God made the Sabbath day for us. The important thing is that all who know Jesus as their Savior should spend time with the family of God on the day they have selected as their Sabbath. I believe that Christ created the Sabbath for man. We read in Genesis that God rested on the seventh day and made that day holy. Man should recognize the Holy Day that God created and set aside to worship and honor Him. I would not want to break fellowship with other Believers because they select Sunday as their Sabbath. The church I pastor has selected Sunday as their day of worship. The bigger question is that no matter what day you have selected as the Sabbath, do you use it to honor God for more than the two-hour service you attend? The book of Mark addresses the subject of the Sabbath for us (Mark 2:27).

I suggest that people get used to going to church every Sunday. I really do understand that committing to church attendance every Sunday can be a challenge. However, look around your neighborhood for a Bible believing church that focuses on learning what God has to say to you and not necessarily to the bells and whistles that are offered. If you have children or grandchildren; sit in their classrooms for a couple of weeks to see if they are being taught the word of God or they are just acting as a babysitting service. Once again, at the risk of repeating myself, our children deserve to hear about their future.

We are now watching the church in America and around the world being persecuted and its numbers being reduced to alarming low attendance. The more our government pushes God back into a closet, the more trouble we experience, not only as a government, but as a family unit. The majority of people are befuddled by what looks like a problem that needs attention, but we have no idea how to approach the problem. We have thrown money at it for years now, but God still says to us, *"be still and know that I am God."* Read…Psalm 46:10

Read – Chapter 1:12-18

John was given instructions to write down what he was about to see so that he could share it with those churches in Asia and churches throughout the centuries. The message he would be writing was to be sent to the churches through the writing that we are reading right now.

The following messages of Revelation Chapter 2-3 were written directly to you and your church. Some might want to say that these churches represent certain dispensations throughout the history of the church. This Revelation was written so that anyone, at anytime, during any century, could pick up the book of Revelation and hold their church up to the standards that Christ has set for His churches. To apply just one church to this century would be a mistake. As you read the cautions given to these various churches, see if these circumstances are prevalent in your home church.

We must be careful when adding certain restrictions to the writings of the Bible. If a church stands on the principles of dispensations concerning these churches, they are in error and should cause you to look at other so-called denominational theories of these same churches.

John was told to write down what he saw and send it to seven specific churches. He was to write this information on a scroll. Scrolls were made in the era of John by using a paper like product coming from a Papyrus plant. Of course, the problem was keeping this product from disintegrating over time. Letters on Papyrus scrolls are still being found in Egypt and other countries with arid climates.

As John turned around, he saw seven golden lampstands surrounding Christ. We now read a description of Christ that matches other descriptions of the Son of God. This description gives us a small insight into the glory of Father God. What an awesome experience for John. Read the description of Christ here in these verses. Don't you get an awesome feeling about whom Christ is? We will read of angels who are dressed in white and have a golden sash around their chest, but we will never read about an angel who has the eyes of Christ as they are described like a burning fire. We do not read about the feet of an angel being described as burning bronze glowing in a hot furnace.

John noticed that Jesus had seven stars in His right hand. The words coming from the mouth of Christ seemed like words that would cut with surgical perfection. All this power of the Throne Room of God is at your disposal as a member of the family of God. Having Jesus as your Savior opens up a new world of what we call "freedom in Christ." I know you have seen very poor people who have little to be happy about, but they have the peace and comfort of the Lord every day. As the Lord becomes your first priority on a daily basis and in everything in your life, you will find more joy and peace than you thought was possible.

John thought that the physical touch of Christ would be fatal, but He found love in the Lord. Once again, Jesus tells John that He is the "First and the Last." Who else in this world or the universe can describe Himself in this way? This description of Christ gives a picture of an all powerful and awesome presence in our lives. Jesus explained that He holds the keys to death and Hades. Jesus has the right over His creation to take life as well as to give life. He tells John that He will live forever, and of course, that eternal life is offered to us. Everyone is guaranteed eternal life. It's either in heaven with God or in hell with Satan. People cannot avoid making a choice because, if they don't make a selection while alive here on earth, one will be made for them by default, and that is always Hell. No one gets a free pass to heaven without acknowledging Christ Jesus as his or her Savior and then living for Him (Ephesians 2:13 / Colossians 1:22 / 1 Peter 1:3).

The Lord explained what John saw as he looked at seven golden lampstands and seven stars. The lampstands represented the seven churches and the seven stars were the angels of the seven churches. John would be writing down information that was to be delivered to those churches. We will read that unless some of these churches straightened up, their lampstand would be removed from the sight of God.

Read – Chapter 1:19-20

John is shown things from the past that emphasize the authority that Jesus had through His Father. He suffered pain when told that Jesus was dead; he rejoiced when he learned Jesus was alive and held the power of life, as well as the keys to death and Hades. There is no escaping the Creator of this world. The question is once again; what will you say to our Lord when our lives are over? I'm sorry was two words that were powerful when we were alive. However, after we die, those two words are useless and are empty.

There are three specific things that John needed to record for the churches in Asia and all future churches.

- "What have you seen"
- "Write what is now"
- "Write what will happen"

It has been demonstrated already that John is speaking with the Lord who has "creation power," and "destruction power" and would soon demonstrate who He was by the use of this mighty power. After this, it would be our decision to accept or reject this awesome power that has love as its foundation. If Jesus has this great power, and He does, would anyone really turn down an opportunity to live forever with the One who will give you all you have ever desired in eternity with your Creator.

We are part of these seven churches. Of course as time has expanded so has the church under Christ. None of us can say that we are the only denomination or church that God blesses singularly. The Lord Jesus is the head of all the Bible believing churches. It is not the church name that dictates who we worship. We worship Christ Jesus and hold up His victory over death as a guarantee that we will have that same victory. As we go along, we will find good attributes as well as negative things that we are guilty of doing ourselves. Our object is not to be critical, but to look in areas where we can improve our personal behavior and change how others see us. Of course, the main object is to experience a relationship with the Lord that is acceptable to Him and will glorify God.

If people would read these verses and understand that God is always looking at their church, I would like to think they would do a better job of being an example of how Christian people live and worship. Although these churches were different geographically, they were all a part of the family of God. If we could just get our individual churches to work together, it would be wonderful. The churches in the days of John had varying cultural differences along with different problems similar to the problems we have in every type of community and church we can think of in today's society.

Look at the background of these churches just for a moment. You will be amazed at just how similar they are to our churches today in practice and belief. Some believe that it was easier in the early days to accept Christ because He was just there on earth and some of them had experienced His miracles of healing the sick and raising the dead. Some even saw Christ die on the cross only to look into an empty tomb three days later as His Father raised Him from the dead. If we will just read the Gospels for awhile, we can see that even the disciples had a difficult time believing what Jesus was doing.

As we begin to look over the churches that were targeted for a message from Christ, it is critical that we plug our church into these seven examples of the early churches. This may be a difficult thing to do because many of us know that we have problems in our churches. However, please look carefully at these examples and learn from their faults.

This commentary is a result of writings over several years of my ministry. After many years of involvement in the Christian church, I have seen a disintegration of the church family. As I visit churches in my community and around the country, a horrible sign of the apathy in the family of God is evident. When walking into a church, I see people in the pews with white hair and mostly women as the bulk of their membership. Men have withdrawn from the church for a myriad of reasons. Some men just cannot stand spending time honoring a God they do not believe in, and have no respect for. Others are just not interested in religion. Of course, many men use this time to take a break from their family. Jesus is the last person on their minds. God holds men accountable for their families maintaining a relationship with Jesus. These men need to read what is about to be revealed through the words of our Lord as it relates to their eternal relationship with Christ. There is a price to pay for turning our back on the God who created us.

I am painfully aware that this trend is now irreversible and represents a part of the arrogance of man and the extreme punishment that will be given to them for eternity. We can read how the events happening in society today aligns with the words of the final eclipse of the human experience. The anxiety we see all around us is the uncertainty of the future. We look at many nations, especially in the Middle East and Europe that are nearing financial collapse. Situational ethics are more prominent today than we have ever seen in our lifetime. However, we need to look back at the history of man and see how he has responded to blessings and curses of God. Wise men seek self-indulgence. Godly men seek forgiveness.

Look at the nature of man when seeing the life of Adam and Eve. They were in the Paradise of God with no worries and only one law and one responsibility. The first was to take care of the grounds. The second was not to eat the fruit of a tree that would cause them to die. Both of these commitments were broken by selfish desires. Today, we have people in the streets of the world's major cities crying out for the rulers of their countries to feed them and take care of their needs. Those who have worked hard for their money must now give it to those who expect others to earn a living for them. There are those who, while no fault of their own, must have help or go hungry. They want more and more from those who have worked hard for what they have. There is a day coming when people will adapt a mindset they deserve help. 2 Thessalonians. 3:10

Related Verses | Mark 24:12-14...*Because of the increase of wickedness, the love of most will grow cold, but he who stands firm to the end will be saved.*

Our responsibility is to get this message out to people in churches throughout America. Let's be responsible for the restoration of these souls who have left the safety of the Savior of the world. We first; however, have to make sure that our relationship with Christ is solid and we are following His will for us as His family.

There is no question that some of you may now feel a sense of urgency about your relationship with God and His Son Jesus as you begin to read what is in store for a world that has become so rebellious against God. The good news is that no matter how bad things become during the next few months or years, you can have a peace that will impress those who are falling apart because of uncertainty. Take this opportunity today to reaffirm your belief in Christ and return to a God that loves you and wants to have a Father-son (or daughter) relationship with you.

Related Verse / Habakkuk **2:3**...*For the revelation awaits an appointed time; it speaks of the end and will not prove false. Though it linger, wait for it; it will certainly come and will not delay.*

The prophet Daniel, along with many of his peers, warned us of the days we are now experiencing. He warns us of the disaster that will someday come upon the world. His advice is to be ready because although it has taken a long time for the words of the prophets to touch us, the time has come for all of us to sit up and pay attention to what is going on around us. We can take the risk of doubting what the prophets and Christ Himself has told us are just stories made up by men, or we can look at all the prophecy that has been fulfilled in the Old Testament and take comfort in the fact that the majority of prophetic events have been fulfilled just as they were prophesied. (Daniel 11:35)

Now that we are finishing up Chapter One of the Book of Revelation, let me ask you a question. Have you read all the referenced Bible verses? I have made a special effort to prove everything I say in this book by using the words of the prophets or Christ. As we get into the later chapters of this book, it will be important that you take the time to look up the Scripture references given after each paragraph. My goal in this book is to teach you to be able to defend the words of the Lord as it relates to the Harvesting of His Saints and His Second Coming.

CHAPTER 2

The Church Age

<u>**Read – Chapter 2:1-7**</u>

The Church at **Ephesus**: (means: "desirable" or "first love")

Ephesus was a well-known capitol and known as the "Light of Asia." Mentioned about twenty times in the New Testament, this city was home base for several well-known early Christians; the Apostles Paul, John, and Timothy just to name a few. The church was on fire for the Lord and their dedication to Him was evident. However, over time the intense love felt for Christ Jesus gave way to the desire to be part and parcel of the social fabric of the city. Believers began to leave the church, and those still involved in the family of God began to lose enthusiasm for serving the Lord.

The location of this city was ideal for trade coming into the western part of Asia Minor. Rivers that snaked their way into the valleys surrounding Ephesus expanded the trade routes even more. A large influx of trading companies and a mixture of cultures made for an interesting, though evil, religious life. The most popular object of worship outside of the Christian church was a goddess called Dianna. The society of this city was made up of wealthy people and people who were known for their wisdom. We know what Jesus had to say about the so-called wise people. They were also known for their desire for wickedness. I guess that is why Jesus told us that the so-called wise people would reject His message. They were too wise for their own good. We must remember that not all people who have money are evil, but those who love their money more than God are in serious danger with the Lord. (Matthew 11:25 / 1 Corinthians 1:19 / 1 Corinthians 1:27)

As we go through each of these churches, please look for a common thread that negatively reflects on the churches to the point that they require a stern warning from the Lord to straighten up or lose their place in heaven. Let me explain what I think is the common thread of negative behavior in these churches, and see if you will agree with me after reading the account for yourself.

God has asked us one thing to do in our life as it relates to our relationship with Him. He said that we should love Him with all our heart, soul, mind, and strength (Mark 12:30). In other words, we need to completely believe in the facts given to us in the Scriptures. I am sure you will agree with me that Christ gives us more love than we return to Him. The fact that He is always there for us, even when we have doubts, gives us encouragement to overcome the pitfalls of life.

Jesus' message to this church was to work hard spreading the Gospel, and continue to be persistent in all that they did for the Lord. Even though it would get physically and emotionally tough to carry on, they were to continue in their loyalty to Christ Jesus. They were asked to despise wickedness, and keep away from its tentacles. It is important to remember that Satan does not need to bother those steeped in sin; he wants to steal Believers from the church of the Lord.

REPENT: If your love has grown apathetic or cold and the Lord has taken a position other than number one in your life, ask for forgiveness, and begin serving God with a new fervor and consistency. Jesus stands ready to help you with a constant love and compassion that only He can give. If you are a mature Believer, please, look around for those who may be hesitant to show their faith and mentor them.

CAUTION: There are people in the Lord's churches that will be removed from His presence if they do not do as they are asked. These are not just idle words from the Christ of God. What He says - He will do! Do we know churches like this? Of course, we do. The caution given by Christ to this church applies to us as well.

Let's look at this church when it comes to loving Him with our entire mind. If our thought life is more and more cluttered with worldly things instead of spiritual things, then can we agree that those things can overwhelm us? Instead of looking to Jesus for help, we look to other things. As we see the worldly thoughts beginning to overtake our thought life, we need to use all the strength God has given us to fight the evil of the world. Jesus has said to us, ask and you will receive whatever you need to fend off evil (Mark 11:24). This church needs to return to their faith in Christ and do the work He asked them to do. It is not easy to stand in front of someone who is hurling insults at us, but we have to get up, get out, and accomplish our mission for Him.

Have we forsaken our first love in Christ Jesus? Do you remember when you first accepted Christ as your Savior as you realized that you were living in sin? You turned all that over to Jesus who died for those sins on the cross. I hope you felt like telling everyone. What a feeling of peace and freedom as the weight of our emptiness in life is alleviated as the weight that overwhelmed us is gone when we understand what Jesus went through to make sure we could spend eternity with Him. Let me encourage you to re-identify the gifts God has given you to serve Him and His church while you are here on earth. If you play a musical instrument for the Lord on Sunday; then play it with all the passion that Christ deserves. If your gift is to share how God touched your body in a healing way, then don't give credit to being fortunate or lucky, but give the credit and glory to God. Christ was there, providing the right physician and the right timing in finding the medical problem. God is found in the smallest details of your life. If you will just step back and look carefully at the troubles you have had, you will see He has been there all the time.

Read – Chapter 2:8-11

The Church at Smyrna: (The Beautiful")

We do not know a lot about the Christians meeting in Smyrna. What we do know is that a strong pagan faction developed in that area and this church would have been under extreme pressure and persecution. In fact, Polycarp was a well-known Believer in this area and was martyred for the church by being burned at the stake. Christ refers to "ten" days of persecution. This is the time some Believers will be tested by Satan and then probably lose their heads. In doing so, they will receive the Crown of Life and spend a 1000 years ruling with Christ in the Millennium. Our goal should be to serve Christ with the gifts He has given us to serve His church.

Now I know that looking into a future that may include persecution that you thought you would never see is a scary idea. However, we must look at the truth of Scripture and try to understand why it is important to learn how we must cope during these times. If you have been told all your life that something called a Pre-Tribulation Rapture event would happen and you would escape persecution and now you see that after reading this book, you indeed will have to go through some of the Tribulation; please, take comfort in knowing that Jesus will be at your side the entire way through the troubles.

You will read in advance about how you will be rewarded as Christ gives all those who have to go through the first two judgments of the Tribulation in Revelation Chapter 20:4-6. These verses, by the way, tell us once and for all and without any question that the First Resurrection has already occurred, and that the Millennium is beginning. Those of us who died prior to this event remain in the Paradise of God and will stay there until the 1000-year period has ended. We were brought to be with Jesus by His angels just prior to the Wrath of God. Once the Wrath of God has been completed God will say, "It is done!" We will await the rest of our family in Christ until they have completed their task for Jesus as He rules with them for the thousand years. Certainly we all can agree that those who die for Jesus during the Tribulation will have earned a right to reign with Christ.

In the United States, it seems as if churches feel a disconnection from the worldwide body of Christ. They hear about the daily persecution of Christians in other countries where evil people continue putting to death those Christians for their faith in Jesus, but it appears they feel that nothing like this could ever happen to them here in the States. This level of persecution toward the Christians may be difficult to understand why God would allow such pain and suffering, but we can see that throughout the Bible, His people have suffered. We forget about the eternal life aspect of Christianity and the eternal peace and love that will follow us through eternity (Revelation 21:4).

There will be no pain, no tears, and no sickness as we live with God in Paradise. Suffering for our Lord is a small price for us to pay, because even in the worst of circumstances, our suffering will be short, after that, we will join Christ for eternity. While we are here on earth Jesus still gives us joy in the midst of troubles.

Related Verse(s) / 1 Peter 1:8-9...*Though you have not seen him, you love him; and even though you do not see him now, you believe in him and are filled with an inexpressible and glorious joy, for you are receiving the goal of your faith, the salvation of your souls.*

God never gives us more than we can handle. When the pressures and persecution increase on us, God steps in and gives us a fresh supply of courage and persistence. God expects us to carry on no matter how much suffering we experience in His name. We must remember that God's wrath will be poured out over the world that has rejected Him. The world in turn rejects us, and they will see to it that we suffer along with them. Many say that God will prevent us from experiencing His wrath, and they are right. We must understand the difference between the Judgments of Christ and God's Wrath. Jesus delivers the "Seal and Trumpet" Judgments, but God's Wrath follows them after the harvesting of the body of Christ. I am sure you will agree that after the way Jesus was treated when coming to this earth with a message of love, only to be met with anger, persecution and death, He deserves to punish this world through His Judgments.

In Matthew 11:28-30, Jesus speak to us about our feeling of exhaustion and the feeling of being weary in our fight against evil forces that want to steal us and our children and grandchildren. We learn in these verses a little of the gentleness of His Spirit and the rest He will give our soul.

Some of the catastrophic illnesses, tragic earthquakes and other physical events of this world could be attributed to the discipline of God as He sees us reject Him. It is not my place to judge or identify a connection between disastrous events coming from God. I will say, however, that the Creator of this world has to be extremely disappointed in the behavior of those He created. Many churches fail to identify these events as a discipline from the Throne Room of God. There are diseases which carry with them a death sentence as an almost certainty. Yet, in this country we have been blessed by the advancement of medicine that in most cases will extend life, if only for a few years. Let's look at the AIDS epidemic around the world. Some have thought this to be a discipline from God for our unchecked immorality. Look how this has affected children. They are innocent lives and they have been given these death sentences because of the selfish actions of mothers and fathers who, for the simple feeling of pleasure, would risk giving a child AIDS. Do we blame God for such a terrible thing or do we look at our own behavior? It does not quite matter where this disease came from but it does matter if our behavior does not change and we continue to throw caution to the wind and kill more of our children. The responsibility of the church is to stand up and profess what is happening in our world because of sin.

Our disdain is not for the people who have AIDS or those who practice homosexuality, but it is for the sin that results from this behavior. In fact, our prayer is that all those who find themselves with this horrible disease will find their way to God who loves them and desires to see them accept His Son as their Savior.

Let's set the record straight about the discipline of God to His people. Revelation 3:19-20 tells us that just like our earthly fathers, God loves us and from time to time we need to receive His discipline. Not because He wants to hurt us, but rather that He loves us so much and wants all of us to make a decision to follow His Son Jesus. Over the years we all have heard what it has taken for some of us to accept Christ as our Savior and begin to follow His lead. Other Believers have been Christians since they were children in grade school. I believe that is the strongest testimony a Believer can have. Not that it has taken a catastrophe for something to happen in our life before we see the light of Jesus. It is not easy to navigate through life maintaining a Christian life. We all need support from our church brothers and sisters.

CAUTION: Be content in your circumstances. Endure the slander that is directed your way. Accept your persecution with boldness and a deep sense of God's power. Replace fear of what is about to happen with peace that is always there from the physical touch of God. Be an OVERCOMER and do not give in to fear.

People may believe that you have gone crazy. Others will know that you are right, but will reject God just to be part of the crowd. Hold on to what you know is right and you will be rewarded in the end. Standing up for Jesus is risky business. We must remember that He stood up for us by suffering death on a cross. His suffering allows us to be forgiven for our sins and to spend eternity with Him in a New Heaven and a New Earth. If you are a Believer and have found to be lacking in your spiritual life, the best time to recommit to the Lord is right this very moment. I know the things I have been talking about are very scary, but you need to read the truth.

PROMISE: Your first death in this world can come at anytime for any reason. Death is no respecter of age, health, wealth, or specific circumstances. Earthly death is a fact that no one can escape. However, there is also another death you can escape; it is called the "second death." This will happen when it is time to give an account for your life to the Creator. Will your life be one filled with glory forever, or with unbelievable torment? It is a very simple choice and for many of us it is an overwhelmingly obvious choice. The second death is for those who do not accept Christ, and is written about in Revelation 20:14-15. You will receive the "Crown of Life" by repenting of your sins and living a life for Christ.

Related Verse(s) / James 1:12…*Blessed is the man who perseveres under trial, because when he has stood the test, he will receive the crown of life that God has promised to those who love him.*

Once again, Jesus speaks to this church about His victory over death. His disciples had a hard time understanding why the Lord was speaking to them of His death and that it was necessary for Him to go through the process. I should point out here that Christ demonstrated His faith in His Father to raise Him from the grave. What would have been the result if Jesus had never come to this earth, and never died for our sins? The answer is that we humans on the earth would have no choice of where our souls would spend eternity. Because of the extreme indescribable love for His creation, God would never allow His creation to be without the choice of returning His love. As God's Son had victory over death by being raised from the dead by His Father, the same will be true of us who believe in the Son, which allows us to be raised with Him. Our victory is even more miraculous than that of Jesus once we accept Him as our Savior. The last breath taken on earth is followed in a nanosecond by your next breath taken as you enter heaven. Jesus had to be separated from God His Father by at least a breath because He had to take on the sin of this world that could not be a part of His Father in heaven.

Read – Chapter 2:12-16

The Church at Pergamum: ("The Citadel")

This city was an ancient hub that was known as the political capitol of that part of the world. It was a city with educated people with their focus on learning. Attention was given to cultural activities and science. We are also told it had an extensive library that was comparable to that of the Alexandrian Library. The gods that were worshipped in Pergamum include Asklepio, Zeus, Serapis, and Demeter. There was also the cult of the emperor. This city made efforts to combine the church and the state into a perfect union. Divide and conquer has been the methodology of Satan since the days of Adam and Eve. Here in this sinful city, the church would come under intense pressure to make a marriage with the city to be as one. Jesus called Pergamum a place where Satan had his throne. Many believers died for their faith in this city. Idol worship, along with the worship of political leaders, identified this city as one that would be used by Satan to destroy Christianity if he could. One Believer that was martyred was a man called Antipas. Jesus called him a faithful witness. Isn't that what you would like to hear from Christ? (Matthew 25:23) God has a special plan for your life. Our responsibility is to ask Him what it is, and then work toward that goal.

CAUTION: As an introduction to this city, Jesus speaks of the "doubled-edged' sword. This implies that Jesus holds a spiritual sword that is used to look into the deepest part of a man, both physically and spiritually. He can separate sin from spiritual commitment without any blurring of the lines. Even as Believers, it is often possible for us to become entangled in sin and lose our way as we try to find our way out of sin. We forget that God looks at us as a whole and holds our words up against our deeds. Jesus also stands ready to forgive sinful behavior and to help put us back on track. We read again about this double-edged sword in the following verse.

Hebrews 4:12... *For the word of God is living and active. Sharper than any underline double-edged sword, it penetrates even to dividing soul and spirit, joints and marrow; it judges the thoughts and attitudes of the heart.*

The Lord implores this church to break away from worshiping false idols. Today, we all believe that there are no idols in our lives, but if we look at our bank accounts, what is in our driveways, and what type of a status we have socially, there can be some areas of our lives that we are treating as if it were an idol. God is saying He wants us to put Him in the number one position of our existence. It should be God, family, and other interests. Of course, getting to that position takes faith and courage as we mature in our relationship with Christ. I am not giving everyone an excuse to be lackadaisical in their Christian life. I am saying that we need to have the Lord on our mind more and more as the years pass in our life. Many new Believers beat themselves up repeatedly as they work out their salvation. We serve a loving God who wants us to live without constant worry about the mountains we have to climb in our life.

Nothing in all creation is hidden from God's sight. Everything is uncovered and laid bare before the eyes of Him to whom we must give account. We will give account for our lives one day, and our Creator will open the book showing everything we have done in our life. Are we ready for that day? If we have continued to ask for forgiveness of the sins we commit, our slate will be wiped clean. However, if we use the loving forgiveness of God to repeat over and over again the same sinful behavior, we should be concerned. (Matthew 10:26)

Stay committed to the name of the Lord. Call upon the Lord's strength to help you to maintain the level of faith you have with Him and to be an encouragement for others around you and to understand the importance of a daily connection with Christ. Keep in mind that Christ desires a deep love relationship with you. The degree of love in your relationship with Jesus will be a barometer of your success as a Believer.

REPENT: There is a group of people within the church who are using the church as a social meeting place and a place where they can spill their evil down the aisles.

Oftentimes, Christianity is not considered to be holy and held in the highest regard. Instead, it is considered a duty and not a relationship with their Savior. These folks are written about in the Scriptures in 1 John 2:18-19... *Dear children, this is the last hour; and as you have heard that the antichrist is coming, even now many antichrists have come. This is how we know it is the last hour. They went out from us, but they did not really belong to us. For if they had belonged to us, they would have remained with us; but their going showed that none of them belonged to us.*

An example of these people in our churches today are those who stay until they cause division in the church and then leave to go on to other churches as a servant of Satan. Jesus speaks of this in the previous verses. The best way to prevent this happening to you is to know the word of God. If you continue learning, no one can deceive you.

Some people have left the security of the Lord and are now participating in worldly activity that threatens their Christianity because of troubles and arguments in the church. This should not be. Some leaders of the church have become overwhelmed by antichrists' within the church whose aim is to always sow discord among the family of the Lord, so that they left the church.

The Nicolaitans are mentioned only a couple of times in the Bible and these references are in the book of Revelation and Genesis. These folks will have an encounter with God and they will be killed and their bodies used as food for the birds of the air. This subject will be spoken of more in future chapters.

These churches are told to repent of the apathy and compromise with the wicked world. If we do not repent, we will be subject to the sword of the Lord. There is hope for all who will be obedient to the Lord.

Read – Chapter 2:17

There is a special place where a magnificent white stone will be placed with your heavenly name on it. No one else will have that name because it will be yours exclusively. The condition for receiving this stone along with the miracle bread of heaven is to overcome evil. One of the great things about being a Believer is enjoying the love that Jesus has for us, and His eagerness to forgive our sin. Pray every evening for your daily behavior, which may have been less than what Jesus expects from you. Keep prayed up and continue to get closer to God by reading His word.

REWARD: Christ will give you some of the hidden manna. Manna was the life sustaining food for forty years while Israel was crossing the desert. It was not just some heavenly food to keep the Israelites from starving while they were in the desert. Manna comes from God and is not only nourishing for the body, but essential for the eternal life of man. It is <u>my opinion</u> that the manna that was picked up every day for forty years had a different heavenly taste each day. There is no basis for this opinion other than the grace and love of God for His chosen people.

In Exodus 16:4 the Lord told Moses that He would cause bread to fall from heaven and that bread would be life sustaining. Note here that the Israelites were given just enough food for a day. That is a great way to live our spiritual lives by living only for today since we have no idea of what will happen the next day.

If you elect to accept Christ as your Savior there will be a new name written in heaven, and it is yours. If you have accepted Him already, Jesus has had your white stone engraved with your special name on it. If you do not know Him as your God who will forgive your sins, then I would suggest you pray to Him right now! All you have to do is ask for the forgiveness of your sins in any words you choose, see Romans 10:9. Then ask someone you know, who knows the Lord, and he or she will help you develop the life plan that Christ has already set out for you.

Read – Chapter 2:18-29

The Church at Thyatira – A Trade City

The church at Thyatira was in a Multi-Cultural city. This town offered several trade services among the clothing industry of the time. Thyatira was also a military town with several deities that were known for violence and war. Within this city was a temple of Dianna. You will remember this goddess when reading about the first city of Ephesus. This was also the home of the infamous Jezebel, who promoted immoral living. In His introduction, Jesus uses a description of Himself. Christ wanted to make sure that this church would have no doubt about who was writing this letter to them. He describes Himself as "the one whose eyes are like blazing fire and whose feet are like burnished bronze." The Son of God leaves no doubt as to His power and strength when sending the message to this church.

Evidently, this church had taken some time to mature in the Lord. They were missing the drive to follow Jesus in every way. This gives us a strong message of how important our deeds are when serving Christ. We will all give an account of our deeds when it is time to explain our service for Him.

PLEASE NOTE: Are you beginning to see a pattern developing here in this part of Revelation? Jesus talks about His love for us and our love and faith that should be in Him. He recognizes our deeds and the service we do in expanding His message. Jesus confirms the fact that He appreciates us doing more for Him as our relationship with Him advances throughout our life. Once we begin to grow in the knowledge of the Lord, our lives become richer and our eyes are opened to the mysteries of the Bible. Many of you know that maturing in the Lord brings peace and confidence in His words.

CAUTION: Once again, apathy and tolerance toward sexual immorality has entered into this church. We see that the Lord has given Jezebel (a prostitute) time to repent of her behavior, but she refuses. Consequently, death and devastation follow her behavior. In our society today, sexual immorality is no longer looked upon as a serious crime against God. In fact, this behavior is expected. One reason for people not to marry is because they fear sexual immorality will eventually infiltrate their marriage. They fear commitment; not because of marriage itself, but their apprehension stems from the fear of infidelity toward one another and the lack of forethought for the years ahead. We know from several studies that it does not make any difference whether they are married or not; infidelity in a relationship has nothing to do with the marriage contract. Sin does not discriminate between the married or non-married. The sexual immorality issue is so strong to resist because the appearance of evil is masked by the ego of "self indulgence." Those who belong to Christ will find the courage to stay away from such behavior with Jesus at their side. It is important to remember that the forgiveness of sin is just a prayer away for the Believer. Many make the mistake of infidelity, but they can repent and receive forgiveness from their mate and especially from God. God asks us to strive for perfection, but none of us can reach that goal. Only God is perfect.

Of course, this reference to Jezebel is an indictment of our country and the world. The United States is hated by many nations because of our acceptance of immoral behavior. We validate this behavior in the name of "freedom of expression," but what we really do is participate in all the sin that sexual immorality brings with it. There are countries that desire this country to be eradicated from the earth because of its immoral behavior. There will be a price to pay for our apathy about this.

King Ahab married Jezebel who was famous for sexual immorality, worshiping Baal, and the making of Asherah poles as idols. King Ahab made an Asherah pole just to make the Lord angry. Jezebel killed all but 100 of the prophets of Israel. She will pay a horrible price for her behavior when the Lord comes for judgment, and so will those who sit on the sidelines without conscience.

Related Verse(s) / 1 Kings 18:4…*While Jezebel was killing off the LORD's prophets, Obadiah had taken a hundred prophets and hidden them in two caves, fifty in each, and had supplied them with food and water.*

Once again, we hear Christ telling us to get in a position to overcome and continue in the faith until He returns. We must become a strong group of "overcomers!" Preparation for the Harvesting of the Saints is vital to this event. The messages to His churches must be taken seriously and with a sense of urgency. Jesus has devoted much of His Revelation explaining the "end times" and what we should do to prepare for this event. Many will say that we need not worry about these times, but you will notice that Jesus does not dismiss His followers from any events before His return for the church. If it is important enough for Him to spend so much time explaining these events, even through His Old Testament prophets, perhaps it is about time that we pay attention to what our Lord is saying to us.

REWARDS: As Jesus has received power to rule over his church, so He will give us authority to rule over nations. There will be a special group of Believers that will rule with Christ for one thousand years (as we will explain later in this study) and usher in an era of peace unknown previously. This is a promise to those who will be going through the Tribulation period. Those who lose their lives for Christ will be given authority to rule with Him for a thousand years.

CHAPTER 3

Balance of Church Prophesy

<u>**Read – Chapter 3:1-6**</u>

The Church at Sardis (Precious Stone)

The church at Sardis was probably as close as we can get to an example of a huge church building that is being built for God. Its sanctuary was being expanded. Its Sunday school departments were growing. The collections were doubling every week and money was no object in their worship of God. There was just one thing missing - life in Christ Jesus!

CAUTION: Nothing can be hidden from God! Jesus speaks about our deeds once again. Are we serving Him earnestly? Do we go to church playing the part of a Believer, and then join with the world's ungodly activities during the week? Are we sharpening our gifts to serve the church of the living Christ? What excuse will we try to use when answering for our lack of deeds done in serving the church?

Related Verse(s) / Hebrews 4:13…*Nothing in all creation is hidden from God's sight. Everything is uncovered and laid bare before the eyes of him to whom we must give account.*

WAKE UP! Please realize that Christ paid a price for your eternal life with Him. He is the giver of life and the One who has the power to take it away. We cannot accept Him and then later reject Him and expect to maintain our heavenly eternal life status. He addresses this issue as He speaks to the church in various verses. Do not be lulled into the idea that you can do anything you wish after accepting Christ without penalty, even at the cost of your salvation. Your name can be blotted out of the Book of Life as referenced in Mark 4:17. We read more about the caution Jesus communicates to us in verses like, Psalm 69:28 and Revelation 3:5.

One example of a specific warning Christ tells us about is found in II John 2:10 that says, *"If anyone comes to you and does not bring this teaching, do not take him into your house or welcome him."* Christ is cautioning us about those who would come to us with a message other than Jesus being the Son of God. We are also told that we can be blotted out of the Book of Life by accepting the words of false prophets. Jesus is not telling us to go hide and live in a commune somewhere out of society. Jesus knows where we have to live and He will give us strength to reject false teaching. Those who believe the Scriptures and tell us to physically retreat from society are wrong. How can we be witnesses for Him if we isolate ourselves? The Holy Spirit has written a balanced guide in Colossians 3:5-10 of how to live our lives as Christians. It is important that we pay attention to the men of God who wrote our Scriptures for the New Covenant, which was established by Christ.

REPENT: Most of us know the way we are supposed to live. We have read how to live a successful Christian life by Biblical principles. Christ has given us an example in 2 John 1:10. We know that we must obey God's word and use the Bible as a guideline for all of us including our family. If we learn to do everything in love and respect for others, then we will be following the Scripture in James 1:22 that says, *"Do not merely listen to the word, and so deceive yourselves. Do what it says!"* Christ brings an unexplainable peace to your life if you will follow His example. It is critical for us to build our religious life on a firm foundation.

When the storms of life come upon us, we will be able to overcome because our foundation is anchored in the word of the Lord. Please, if you are not serving the family of God with your gifts, begin doing it right now by calling your pastor and volunteering to help. We have a huge job right at this very moment for the church to get excited again about what they will soon see in heaven. If we are living for only what the world gives us, then we are indeed a sad commentary on what Christ wants us to be.

Sure, I want to enjoy the things of life, but only those things that are given to me by the Savior. When I was a young man, I wanted everything in the world, no matter what the cost. I found out much later that there is no greater gift than the opportunity to work for the God who created me. I hope and pray that you have discovered this as well.

REWARD: Those who overcome will walk clothed in white with the Lord. Their name will <u>never be blotted out</u> of the Book of Life, and they will receive special recognition before God the Father. This should be every Christian's goal. This is what life is all about. We are here on this earth for just a whisper of time when compared with eternity. We need to act like a people who have already overcome the world.

Related Verse(s) / James 4:14 speaks to us as we navigate through our life. Please look for ways that will be pleasing to God. A lifetime seems forever when we are twenty, but when we reach sixty-five, life seems so very short. I know I speak for many people out there who agree with me and feel the same pain for our children and grandchildren who are unaware of the shortness of life, and are not preparing for the end.

It is true that our life compared with eternity is but a wisp of air. It is so important that we give one hundred percent when using our gifts to serve God. It will not be long before all of us will be giving an account of our life. It is easy to put God on the back burner of our life as a Believer, especially if we are younger, but time has a way of slipping by, and without warning, it is time to meet our Creator.

Read – Chapter 3:7-13

The Church at Philadelphia: ("Brotherly Love")

Of all the "Seven Churches", many Christians believe their church is most like this one. This church receives praise from Christ Jesus and promises that for the "sake of the elect" the Tribulation Period will be cut short. This has been badly translated to mean that the church will not have to suffer the persecution of the Tribulation. First, this church is no longer alive. All of its members long ago died and hopefully are in the Paradise of God. Like today, this church probably lived through a younger generation that continued to worship Christ throughout the area. Secondly, if as some say, that these churches are dispensational, then this church is only a part of history and nothing from this church carries over into all the years following. You can see the misguided process of this thought.

They were given a task of spreading the word of God and could not retreat. This church was a group of Christians in a Greek culture. Just what does that special promise of God cover, and why just to them, not the other churches? There is no such promise directly to this church regarding a free pass to heaven prematurely. Since all of these churches are examples for us as we participate in our local churches today, we see outlines of seven early churches that help us to understand the problems involved in our relationship with the Leader of our Church, Christ Jesus. This church acts as an example of what our church should already be doing.

Although there is a special promise for those who keep on serving God, it applies to all churches that will conform to the attributes of the Church of Philadelphia. This particular church faded from existence, but they left us a great lesson of persistence. The promise for all the Believers during the time of Tribulation is that if it were not for the church, the Tribulation would continue much longer. The church will be harvested by the angels of our Lord prior to the wrath that will be given to the balance of people left on earth. This subject will be covered more in Chapter Eleven. We will be preparing to be united with the Lord and be brought together to meet Jesus before the seven bowls, or vials, are poured out on the earth as the Wrath of God. Woe to anyone who tells others that for some reason they will not have to go through the Tribulation. This doctrine is heresy. It will be the cause of the "Great Falling Away" of those who will be devastated when learning that they were not caught away, but are still here when crisis turns to chaos. Seek out the truth of the Scriptures and be at peace with what you find.

Matthew 24:10-11... *At that time <u>many will turn away from the faith and will betray and hate each other</u>, and many false prophets will appear and deceive many people.*

ENCOURAGEMENT: Jesus recognizes the good deeds of this body of Believers. He understands that they are extremely tired from their efforts, but He states that they must continue sharing the Gospel of Christ Jesus and never deny His name. Christ will make all those who thought they were Jews, but were liars, come and bow down at His feet. There is a word of caution here and that is not to deny the name of Jesus.

OPEN DOOR: Here God is sharing a witnessing principle for us. Even though we may often tire of presenting Christ to others and living a different lifestyle because of our belief in Him, the Lord will keep unlocking doors for us that we must open, no matter how tired we are. He is saying; listen, I know you are exhausted, but I am going to keep your witnessing door open so that you can share with others that I am still alive, and that denying my name is a fatal error. Jesus says that if we bring just one soul destined for the Lake of Burning Sulfur back into fellowship, it will result in many of our sins being forgiven (James 5:20).

This church was a hard working group of Believers. Their own physical strength had been tested. When they combined their physical strength with their spiritual power, they formed a foundation that added to the cause of Christ. They still held their ground when witnessing to others saying, "Christ Jesus is Lord." They knew that people had to approach God with a repentant heart and confess that Jesus is the Son of God; not a very easy thing for a Jew to do in those days or, as a matter of fact, for anyone in these days. Can we compare ourselves to those who witnessed as this church did? In today's time, would we say that our witnessing efforts are comparable to other so-called churches that pervert the word of God? Every one of us will answer for our opportunity to tell others about Christ, but then elected to keep silent. Don't let that be you!

PROMISE: Since these Believers, and by the way, you as well, have kept Gods commands and have endured patiently, professing the name of Christ Jesus; you will be spared the "Wrath of God" that is surely coming to pass. I would suggest that we do not use this message to determine if we will experience a pre-tribulation rapture of the church. You can take comfort that the Wrath of God will not be directed at Believers. The Tribulation will be no bed of roses, even for the true Believer, but God has promised to cut those days short for us. When we read of the last three and a half years of the Tribulation period, we should be prayerful that the Lord will have already harvested His church. The church was promised a shortened Tribulation period. It is spiritually immature to believe that Christ is promising His church an early departure from this world before the Tribulation. The lesson for the church is to overcome all the persecution it will receive during the Tribulation period. The church will take great comfort in knowing that they will be seeing their Savior soon. (Matt. 13:21 / Mark 4:17 / Rev. 11:15-19)

CAUTION: As well as God perceives this church; He is saying the same thing to them as the others. You must become a group of overcomers. We have to hold on to what we have in Christ. Do not let Satan or anyone else steal your Crown of Life. Here in this country we seem to feel that God looks at us in a special light; when in fact, He has to look at us at times as miserable failures in our attempt to live a life that reflects the Love of God.

REWARD: You will have a pillar with your name on it in the "New Jerusalem." You will be identified by a special mark with the name of God, and the new city in which you will reside. You will have a personal relationship with Jesus that has reached a level of a truly natural born son or daughter. Your name can never be changed because you are now a part of eternity in the family of God. You have been sealed as a family member of the Living God.

Related Verse(s) / Ephesians 4:30… *And do not grieve the Holy Spirit of God, with whom you were sealed for the day of redemption.*

Do yourself a favor and do not be led astray by those who would scoff at spending an eternity with Christ. Many people around you would like nothing better than to see you abandon your faith. Moving away from Christ would endorse their evil behavior. Sinners think that somehow there will be a group of their friends in the Lake of Burning Sulfur, and they will sit around and talk about the good old days. There will be no rest from the torment that will last for eternity. There will be no chance in the future to change your mind and to be brought back to peace and safety. The fact is, these people will be alone and only able to hear the billions of people around them screaming in pain and calling out for mercy. The pain and suffering will not stop - ever. We can scream this warning at the top of our voices, but most people will not listen.

Read – Chapter 3:14-22

The Church at Laodicea: (So called "Today's Church.")

This is not a very popular church to be compared with. Of course, if you believe that this church represents your church today, then there is reason for worry. We have to keep reminding ourselves that Christ, when talking about the churches, is not talking about a building as a church, but a group of His believers throughout the world throughout all generations. Many believers sitting inside churches have strayed so far from the will of God that this warning from Jesus should be taken urgently. Jesus has devoted many words explaining to us what our churches should look like and how we are to act. If you make the mistake of not looking at every one of these churches as examples for our behavior in Christ, then you are risking missing the message to you and your church family.

CAUTION: Some think their salvation is all wrapped up in a package that cannot be taken back. They think they can get away without having to share the salvation message with others. They also believe they can ride the fence or hide in the safety of their homes without utilizing the gifts God has given them to serve Him. And perhaps the worst thing of all, do you really believe that belonging to a certain denomination or church automatically qualifies you for heaven? In the past, here in the United States, people have died and gone on to be with the Lord without having to endure extreme persecution. You may not have to endure such persecution. I think many of those who are young today should live with the knowledge that it is possible for some to be alive when the Tribulation begins. Today, the world lives on the edge of disaster. Any day can mean we will be caught in a terrorist plan that will end our lives (2 Thessalonians 5:3). Jesus warns us of a day coming soon that will be far worse than a terrorist attack. The destruction will be devastating and many lives lost. There is a way out of this devastation.

The Book of James tells us of how our lives should be involved in the life of Christ. You will quickly find out that it is not your denomination that will guarantee your entrance to heaven. Only the grace of God and your obedience in following Him will give you eternal life with Him. In other words, don't just talk the talk, walk the talk! I am sure you will agree with me that a close relationship with Christ makes these times more tolerable and joy can be experienced no matter what the circumstances. There is nothing more important than keeping our eyes on Jesus and following His commands.

In the Book of Galatians (5:22-23), we read some of the attributes of the Holy Spirit living within us. If we rely on the Spirit God gave us, we are ready to battle anything. There is joy, peace, and yes, patience given to us. Which of us would reject self-control, gentleness, and a life filled with the goodness and faithfulness of our God? I pray that this verse is exciting for you to read and to live by.

There is no doubt that Christ Jesus expects us to accept Him and then take action. There is a cost of discipleship. We know that there is nothing we can do to deserve salvation, but there is something we must do to serve the Lord. Arguing over these things is what we call "milk issues." Most of you should be beyond the part of the basic principles of God. If you have accepted Christ, then you accepted ALL of Him. You are expected to work for Him with the talents He has already given you. If you decline to obey Him, you may be in serious trouble.

CAUTION: Wealth has blinded many to the truth. Those who have an insatiable appetite for money usually are the unhappiest people. They soon discover that money does not buy happiness or peace of mind. Our churches today feel that the more money we can throw at a building fund to make it bigger, the more people we can lead to Christ. I have heard statistics over the years that only seven percent of those who attend church were "saved" in the church. Personal evangelism brings more people to Christ than any other form of ministry.

I am afraid that the more money we get, the less we serve God. Oh yes, there are many ministry outreaches formed by the church, but the same twenty percent of the people who normally serve in the church are doing most of the outreach. We have received the message that giving money to the church is somehow the foundation of our ministry. Nothing could be further from the truth. Many can give large sums of money, but spend little time in the ministries they fund. Some people believe the more money they can give for public outreach, the less they physically have to do with respect to using their talents for God. Money is not a talent, using it properly is. God does not need our money. He wants you to become involved in His ministry. He is the one who opens doors for the planting of His seed in others. God will provide those whom He has blessed with the gift of making money, but the money is not the gift meant to replace their talents.

Related Verse(s) / <u>1 Timothy 6:10</u>…*For the love of money is a root of all kinds of evil. Some people, eager for money, have wandered from the faith and pierced themselves with many griefs.* As I mentioned earlier, money itself is not bad; the love of it is evil.

God has given that same person, or persons, talents that only they have been assigned. Therefore, please do not say that your gift to God is money. It was His to begin with. He wants your personal service toward Him to show where your heart is. Support your church and make sure your pastor is not in need. But do the will of God in your life! Be a disciple of Christ! Focus your efforts on the One who will give you Paradise forever. The problem here with the rich man is that he may worship his money over the Savior. Oftentimes money corrupts. Almost all of those who win lottery millions are broke within a couple of years of receiving their money. Money can corrupt to the point where it is an idol.

REPENT: God loves us, and because He does, He corrects us just as you do with your children. We know when we have been wrong, so let's repent of the sin of mediocrity and apathy, and catch on fire for Christ. He is waiting for you to answer Him this very moment. Let Him into your life for fellowship and love.

Related Verse(s) / Proverbs 3:12…*because the LORD <u>disciplines</u> <u>those he loves</u>, as a father the son he delights in.*

REWARD: Be an "overcomer". Earn the right to sit with your Father at the throne of grace and power. Assure yourself an opportunity to be with Christ Jesus for eternity. Most of all, tell others about the love you have found with Christ. This is especially important for your family. Not one of us desires to spend eternity without them. Live as examples of the children of God.

If you believe that these seven churches mentioned here are in chronological order representing only the past churches throughout the centuries of old, then you have major reason for despair. You would be missing the admonition of Jesus to our churches. These were statements of love to the churches. They were meant to be part of the eternal kingdom of God. You need to hear all that Christ has to say to these churches and then change your life to comply with what the Lord expects of you!

Here is an example of what some think these churches were. These churches are supposedly aligned in eras referred to as dispensations. Oftentimes, when faced with subjects that challenge our imagination, we stray from the counsel of the Holy Spirit and make assumptions that are wrong. The problem is if we are wrong, spiritual lives can be threatened.

1. **Ephesus:**
   The first church in the first century. Gets caught up in ceremony and departs from their first love…Christ Jesus.

2. **Smyrna:** (92-315)
   This church brings us martyrs who are dying for Christ.

3. **Pergamum:** (315-500)
   A church that has made a decision to join with the state in a one-world church.

4. **Thyatira:** (500-1500)
   Suffers extreme persecution of the church during the middle ages.

5. **Sardis:** (1500-1700)
   The reformed church. Steeped in tradition and pageantry, but short on deeds.

6. **Philadelphia:** (1700-1900)
   This was a missionary church with emphasis on ministry outreach and the expansion of God's kingdom.

7. **Laodicea:** (1900-present)
   Many believe that this is the church of today.

Churches today reflect both the positive and negative aspects of these Seven Churches, none of which were abandoned by the angels assigned to them by God. God still has His angels stationed in our churches. If you have a church that is experiencing any of these problems, take the lead and begin to move in the direction Jesus wants you to go.

If we as a church will just get down on our knees together, Christ will honor that and begin to heal our differences. Don't worry about the differences; focus on getting closer to the Lord. Stop trying to make excuses for God because some men cannot understand or make sense of things mentioned by the Holy Spirit in these passages.

Before going on to Chapter Four and beyond, I need to insert a common belief among some churches who believe that not everything written beyond this point was written to the church of today. They are quick to say that the church is not specifically mentioned after Chapter Four. This same group of people insists that the book of Matthew was written more for the Jews than today's Gentile Believers. If we were to cut out all the books, chapters, and verses of the Bible supposedly written to one specific group of people, our Bibles would be significantly smaller.

There are many people in our time trying to neutralize the words written in the Bible. Many of you will be reading this at a time that has been very challenging for Believers. Christians have left the church and have actually turned on the God they once professed. Others have just quit going to church for reasons they say are politics, backbiting, hypocrites, and other sins of the church family. Please remember this; there is a "miracle man" coming on the scene in a short time. Many of you will think that perhaps Jesus changed His plans and returned to earth to bring peace for the world.

There is a good reason why God requires that we read His words and the words of His Son on a daily basis. Jesus paid a horrible price for us to have an eternal future with Him in a setting that looks as if it were the Garden of Eden. We need to read His words and obey them.

Do many church members believe that John was miraculously taken to heaven to write down all that would take place during the last few years called the Tribulation to just seven churches that for the most part have disbursed? The warnings of Christ to the Seven Churches are warnings we, the church now, must take to heart.

If you are one of those people who believe in the doctrine of dispensations concerning these churches, I am glad you are reading this book. I can only pray that you will remember this book and realize that perhaps the Bible is right. What you are about to read speaks to the events during the Tribulation. Pay serious attention to what Christ is saying. Your eternal life in on the line.

The Tribulation
The Judgments of Christ
The Seal and Trumpet Judgments

* CHAPTER 7 HAS BEEN RELOCATED TO THE NEXT SECTION FOR INSTRUCTIONAL PURPOSES

CHAPTER 4

The Throne Room

Read – Chapter 4:1-2

The door to heaven is always open for those who are seeking Christ, but this was a special event. Here, Christ is inviting the "soul" of John to enter the heavenly Throne Room. Please understand that it was the spirit of John that went through this door and not his body. Flesh and blood cannot inherit the Kingdom of God. (1 Corinthians 15:50) No sinful thing can enter the Throne Room, therefore only the spirit of John could enter. John's soul or spirit is what entered heaven. If John's body were to enter the Throne Room, he would not be able to return to earth, because he would receive a heavenly body to replace the sinful body he lives in on earth. That is not to say that John was full of sin, but that he still has a sinful nature, which is unacceptable to be in heaven (Matthew 26:4; Galatians 5:17). The only sinful thing that approaches God on a daily basis is the evil one called Satan. He approaches God often to get permission to tempt man (See the book of Job). This coming and going of Satan from earth to the Throne Room will end very soon, and just as the door to heaven will be closed to Satan, it will be closed forever for those who do not accept Christ (Rev. 12:7-8).

We read in 1 Corinthians 15:50 that mere flesh and blood cannot enter heaven. Even though you and I have been born again, we are not purged of the evil human nature that stays with us. That is why the Bible says that our flesh is always fighting the Holy Spirit within us

(2 Peter 1:4). If you have complied with Romans 10:9, you have the Holy Spirit within you and He will fight and give you the strength to overcome evil's lure.

We know by reading the Book of Job that Satan was given permission to test Job. The only restriction was that Satan could not kill him. Satan enters heaven everyday as he moves around the world stalking vulnerable Believers to challenge their convictions. If we go through life expecting evil to attack us, it is easier to acknowledge the attack and call on the strength of the Lord through the Holy Spirit to assist us in our challenge.

I hate to stop right here but it is important that we look at a few instances of men looking into heaven to get a feel for the type of communication that God used with His servants. Let's take the time to look at other times in the Scriptures when the <u>door to heaven was</u> opened.

In Ezekiel 1:1, Heaven was opened up so Ezekiel could see what was going to happen in the immediate future and what events would be taking place in the long-term. Ezekiel was not taken up to heaven, as John would experience later, but saw visions in his spirit. John's spirit was taken into heaven to actually see the visions of the future through the eyes of Christ Jesus.

Neither, by the way, was John's body dead as he witnessed the final days of man and this earth. In the case of John, his heart was beating, but his soul or spirit was with the Lord. That is important to note because some people want to use the first verse or two when making a case for a Pre-Tribulation Rapture. I know, it doesn't make any sense to me either, but people will do all they can to prove a point, even if they are in error. If we take just one verse out of their rapture equation, their whole system begins to crumble. It is so important that we read Scripture critically; that is, word by word and verse by verse. Heaven was opened up in the vision of Ezekiel. John experienced a unique situation in that his soul or spirit entered the Throne Room of God.

We see heaven opened up once again in the baptism of Christ Jesus. The message from heaven emphasized the Son of God submitting to baptism and the pride that was felt by His Father as Jesus came up out of the water. From the Throne Room of God came the Holy Spirit that would dwell with Christ just as He does with us.

The baptism of Christ gives us a view of heaven opening up and God demonstrating to the world that He was pleased that His Son became obedient to baptism. It is so sad to see some denominations see baptism as an option to be performed at their convenience. To see baptism as merely an option and not a part of the "Born Again" process demonstrates a lack of respect for Christ.

Stephen saw heaven opened up and standing there beside God was Christ Jesus. The spirit of Stephen was no doubt in the process of going to Paradise while being stoned and that is where he is today and will be there until Christ's return. All those who belong to Christ through being "born-again" and who have died are with Steven today as they wait for the return of Christ for His Church (Acts 7:55-56).

Jesus has given us these examples to support our belief in what the Scriptures say about heaven. We are not looking forward to some sort of fairy tale land; we know heaven to be an actual place where we will be a resident some day.

The last case I will mention is the time when heaven was opened up for the Apostle Peter. Peter was about to be challenged to give the Gospel message to everyone who would listen, both Jew and Gentile. He was about to be given a hunger for souls to be added to the family of God by teaching the Gentiles. It was important that Peter understood just who that family was. The lesson here was that all people deserve to hear the "Good News" of the Christ of God. You and I have accepted the responsibility to spread the word. As you read the complete story of Peter in these verses, you will understand the message more thoroughly (Acts 10:10-13).

Related Verse(s) / Acts 10:10-11...*He saw heaven opened and something like a large sheet being let down to earth by its four corners.*

BACK TO OUR TEXT

Read – Chapter 4:3

At this point in the second verse we are looking at Father God. Two jewels are described for us. Jasper is believed to be a stone that emits many colors, but its most outstanding color is the color of fire. Carnelian is a gem that has a brilliant red color. There would be no question as a person looks at its quality of pure color that this gem would be a favorite of God. Carnelian is part of a wall in the New Jerusalem. Both of these stones are considered very hard which demonstrates strength. The Throne Room of God has been described as a wonderful place with an unsurpassed beauty. It brings together all the colors of a magnificent rainbow that could only be in heaven.

The Throne Room was encircled by brilliant colors. The picture of that had to hypnotize John for an instant. We have seen many beautiful rainbows in our day, but nothing that could compare with the enormous array of colors reflecting the awesomeness of God. The array of brilliant colors when seen in a sequence pattern can sometimes cause people to have what we would call a seizure. In this case, the colors were a picture of an awesome God that man would have a hard time even looking at. Everything we read about the Throne Room of God and His Temple exemplifies the power and brilliance, not only the mind of God, but of His glory in the vast expanse of color in His kingdom. This same power and glory is available for us as we prepare to meet Jesus.

Read – Chapter 4:4-6a

We could spend pages trying to identify these elders around the throne. It would seem to me that God would desire to have the most honorable men who have demonstrated a life of spiritual purity and obedience. John saw this event at a time when the Tribulation was about to begin. The best many people can come up with when describing the twenty-four Elders is these men are comprised of the Twelve Apostles and the head of the Twelve Tribes of Israel. Of course, John would be one of the Apostles in their theory, but he is being shown what is to happen and perhaps his seat is being overlooked by the desire of God. Once again, we are left to wonder what the meaning of this mystery is, and it will only be solved when we get to heaven.

Can you get the picture of the power of the Throne of God? Lightening and peals of thunder show us the immense power of the Godhead loaded with color so impressive that only God could create. By the way, that power of the Throne is available to you and me as we walk with Christ through this earthly life. Keep this mental picture of heaven as you read through the Revelation of the Christ of God. On top of all this color around the throne was the amplified effect of what appeared to be a sea of glass that was perfectly clear. What a beautiful picture this brings to our minds eye! The pure clear glass represents the purity of the Throne Room.

Read – Chapter 4:6b

There is a lot of symbolism written here when describing the four creatures surrounding the throne. We could spend many hours attempting to identify exactly what these creatures represent. However, we will not do that here in this study, but will give you a quick overview of these creatures. Then we will accept what God has shown us and be satisfied that one day we will know for sure what these creatures represent. We are told that they were covered with eyes, which represent an all-seeing God. Nothing can be hidden from God, nor does He forget anything unless it is a request to have our sins forgiven.

As I mentioned in the paragraph above, there can be nothing hidden from God. I know that flies in the face of some who think they are so clever, they can outwit God, but to their dismay when accountability comes, they will be sadly mistaken. Everything, and the Scriptures mean everything; will be opened up for us to see as we answer to Christ for our behavior. I doubt that we will say anything back to Christ as He reminds us of our behavior on earth. This has to make most of us who believe that Jesus is indeed the Son of God, take a sigh of relief as we remember that all of our sins have been forgiven. However, we may have to be a little nervous when He sees our good works that should have been done in the Name of the Father when we were on earth. (Hebrews 4:13)

The Throne Room Creatures

Read – Chapter 4:7-8

Creature 1

We will look at the face of a lion mentioned here and search to see the application and similarities that could represent these creatures in the Throne Room setting. Besides having eyes all over its body, which represent an all-seeing God, its worship of God was pure and true. There are over 80 references to a lion in the New International Version of the Bible. Most of those references tell us of the power of the lion and the position the lion carries on this earth. Verses explaining the great power of the lion are no coincidence when looking at this creature around the throne. Our first reference will show the incredible power of this beast, (Numbers 23:24). This power combined with the ability to see everything, and that nothing can be done in secret anywhere, is breathtaking. The next reference verse will speak of the craftiness of the lion and an example of how crafty Satan can be when stealing Believers from the safety of the Great Shepherd. Now we are reading that a creature like a lion is worshiping and serving God. The vicious creature we all know has become an ultimate creature in service to the Godhead.

1 Peter 5:8-9...*Be self-controlled and alert. <u>Your enemy</u> the <u>devil prowls around</u> like a roaring lion looking for someone to devour. Resist him, <u>standing firm in the faith</u>, because you know that your brothers throughout the world are undergoing the same kind of sufferings.*

<u>Creature 2</u>

The second creature has the face of an ox. What is so special about an ox, you might ask. An ox is often mentioned as an animal for sacrifice. An ox was also critical for the everyday work that was needed to assure a crop. Oxen were, and are still today, used in some countries to do the heavy everyday tasks that guarantee food for families. An ox will continue to pull a load until it drops. It will not stop if it is just tired. This certainly would represent persistence of the Lord of Lords. The strength of the ox is undisputed as the beast providing food for nations, both as crops and even for the meat on its bones. We often see them in wildlife programs being pursued by several lions, tigers, etc., and we see that oftentimes it takes several natural enemies to take them down. When combining all the attributes of the lion and then adding those of the ox, we see the creatures around the throne as adding to the complete picture of the Godhead.

When combined with the capability to see all things this power and persistence represented by the ox is magnified beyond description. God never gives up on you and me. He will have fellowship with us for eternity. If we deny Him, He will also be just as determined to see us face judgment for our disobedience.

Related Verse(s) / Psalm 22:21…*Rescue me from the mouth of the lions; save me from the horns of the wild oxen.*

Proverbs 14:4…*Where there are no* **oxen***, the manger is empty, but from the strength of an ox comes an* <u>*abundant harvest*</u>. The Lord refers to the "Harvesting" of His Believers immediately after the last trumpet has been sounded. There is no surprise that the power of the oxen is represented around the throne. I look forward to the day that we will see the power of God in person.

Creature 3

Now we come to the creature that has the face of a man. All of these creatures were created by God to serve Him. All of these creatures represent power and magnificence. They were also created to love their Creator both on earth and in heaven. This symbol of created man is very interesting as being one of the four creatures in the Throne area of God. This creature with the face of man could represent the awesome awareness of what man could have experienced, as he became part of the Throne Room. When combined with the ability to see all things that could get in the way of worshiping God, we can see where man should be, and not where he is today. Adam was created to have fellowship with God without reservation, so too is this creature, and so too are we. Man will always be a part of the Throne Room of God.

Jesus created man in His image and the image of the Godhead; that is the Father, Son, and Holy Spirit. He was created to have a special relationship with the Lord. How could man be absent from the creatures serving around the Throne? Man was meant to worship God without reservation. He was meant to be a willing servant for the glory of God. Man was to be a jewel in the crown of God.

Related Verse(s) / Deuteronomy 4:32… *Ask now about the former days, long before your time, from the day God created man on the earth; ask from one end of the heavens to the other. Has anything so great as this ever happened, or has anything like it ever been heard of?*

Creature 4

The fourth and final creature had the face of a flying eagle. We all know the ability to be free and to soar above all things as the empire of the air is given to the eagle. Now we give the eagle the ability to see all things that makes this bird a magnificent king of all that is below him. No one could have better protection than an eagle flying over him. When adding eyes all around this creature he becomes a fierce protector of the Throne Room of God. The eagle's freedom should be an example of the freedom we have in Christ.

Related Verse(s) / Hosea 8:1… *"Put the trumpet to your lips! An eagle is over the house of the LORD because the people have broken my covenant and rebelled against my law.*

Summary

Now I know that we could get into a deeper, more spiritual meaning of these four creatures. It is more important to see that serving God should be the focus of all men. The following shows us the focus these creatures have on worshiping God. This determination and focus encourages others to do the same as we see the creatures' effect on the elders. Our relationship with Jesus must serve as an example for others when looking toward heaven for answers. We are challenged to the limit of our ability to see these creatures in the mind's eye, but do not get dismayed.

Read – Chapter 4:9-11

It should be noted here that God is the <u>TRUE</u> God. He has tried to let us know about His attributes. In these cases, He has used man and beast to show His power and authority. He created the earth and ALL that is in it, and thereby has to answer to no one for His decisions, nor His sovereignty over what He has created. We follow Him and obey Him because He is God and there is no other. Accepting this fact is hard for many to get a grip on, but nevertheless, He is the One in complete authority over this earth. He can, and will, destroy it whenever He has predestined that to happen.

PLEASE NOTE: Many Believers think that Chapter 4 through Chapter 22 is not for the churches. They feel that because a specific church is not mentioned again, they believe that everything written beyond this point is for someone else and certainly not them. What a pitiful position for those who are confessing Jesus as the Christ of God to say that the next nineteen chapters are for someone else. This is another rapture equation. If we add just this one verse to their theory, their whole system continues to crumble.

Related Verse(s) / Revelation 22:16... *I, Jesus, have sent my angel to give you this testimony for the churches. I am the Root and the Offspring of David, and the bright Morning Star."*

Both Jews and Gentiles are offered the gift of Salvation to them by the Messiah. I want to be clear that this is not written as an indictment to those who believe in some sort of Pre-Tribulation Rapture event. My prayer is that they will read this and keep it stored away in their memory as the antichrist comes on the scene. What is written in the entire book of Revelation is for both you and me, right this very moment, even if you are reading this in the year of 2100 or later.

CHAPTER 5

Who Is Worthy

Read – Chapter 5:1

Here is an amazing verse that tells us that God the Father, at least on this occasion, appeared to take on the image of a man. I guess this shouldn't be so amazing since He told us in the beginning of Genesis that man was created in the image of the Godhead (Father, Son, and Holy Spirit). We are also told that God is a spirit in John 4:24; yet, here we read in our first verse that John saw in the right hand of the Father a scroll written on both sides. We know that God has described Himself as a Spirit many times, but this time He has taken on a form similar to the heavenly body of Jesus. What difference does this make and is it worthwhile to discuss? We must learn not to limit the Godhead no matter what the situation. I have no doubt that Father God is primarily Spirit as we are told in the Gospel of John. We would be wise not to limit Father God, Christ Jesus Himself, or the Holy Spirit.

God is preparing to hand over all authority for the "End Time" events. On this scroll was the plan for the end of the world as He had created it. Remember that only God the Father knows the time when this will happen. Now He is getting ready to pass this information over to His Son, who has paid the price to obtain taking the scroll and the authority to carry it out as His Father intended. Of course, Jesus knew what His Judgments and the Wrath of God would be; however, He did not know the day it would begin. We who have been in the religious world for some time have known that our time here on earth is limited.

Related Verse(s) / <u>Ephesians 1:22</u>…*And God placed all things under his feet and appointed him to be head over everything for the church, which is his body, the fullness of him who fills everything in every way.*

It appeared at first that no one was qualified and had earned the right to open this scroll. Was John being told that no one was found worthy to open the scroll? This scroll was written before the world was created. There is no question that the scroll should have been very fragile, but just as God had His chosen people wander in the desert for 40 years without wearing one fraction of an inch from the soles of their sandals, so the scroll was protected by the hand of God. Every one of the Judgments of Jesus was sealed on this scroll before He came to earth, to offer Himself as an ultimate sacrifice for sin. God has not been surprised by anything man has done in the past, nor will He be stunned by what man does in the future. We know that God is the only One who knows when the Tribulation will begin and when the Judgments and Wrath will be given.

Related Verse(s) / <u>Mark 13:32-33</u>… *"No one knows about that day or hour, not even the angels in heaven, <u>nor the Son,</u> but <u>only the Father</u>. Be on guard! Be alert! You do not know when that time will come.*

The Lamb of God was and is worthy for worship by those around the throne and to open the seals on the scroll. This scroll contains much more than just judgments. It contains the sentence for the world that rebelled against God's Son. It was God's desire that all people would accept Him as God, and His Son as the Savior of the world. Because God knows all things, it does not make it any easier for Him as He sees the human beings He created reject Him outright without any concern.

<u>Read – Chapter 5:2-5</u>

Who was this mighty angel proclaiming the question? Mighty angels are mentioned quite often now, as we get further into the book of Revelation. They will play a crucial role in the events of the Tribulation Period. Angels have always been busy doing the will of God, but now as the end is drawing near; they are utilized more and more. In this situation, the angel is not identified. We will, however, read about mighty angels in other sections of Revelation and previous books of the

Bible. One of these angels was mentioned when revealing the birth of John the Baptist: recorded in Luke 1:19

Zechariah was told that his wife would bear a child in her old age and he was skeptical. This angel closed the mouth of Zechariah until John the Baptist was born. All that Gabriel predicted to Zechariah came to pass and demonstrated the power of God (Luke 1:8-19). We will become more familiar with Gabriel as we continue through the book of Revelation.

We must understand the position of angels in the heavenly realm. There are different tiers of angelic power used by God. Some angels are identified as "mighty angels," others are called "special angels," and some as just angels. We should see that angels can be given enormous power over certain situations. Angels were there at the tomb opening of Christ to tell His followers that He had risen. All of those who know Christ as their Savior have been assigned angels to watch over them, (Psalm 91:11). In the Book of Revelation, we read about the activity of angels in almost every chapter.

NOW BACK TO OUR TEXT IN REVELATION

Read – Chapter 5:6

Who is worthy to open the seven seals? There was only One who had paid the price to break the seals on the scroll. The information that was c further into the book of Revelation. They will play a crucial role in the events of the Tribulation Period. Angels have always been busy doing the will of God, but now as the end is drawing near; they are utilized more and more. In this situation, the angel is not identified. We will, however, read about mighty angels in other sections of Revelation and previous books of the Bible. One of these angels was mentioned when revealing the birth of John the Baptist: recorded in Luke 1:19

Zechariah was told that his wife would bear a child in her old age and he was skeptical. This angel closed the mouth of Zechariah until John the Baptist was born. All that Gabriel predicted to Zechariah came to pass and demonstrated the power of God (Luke 1:8-19). We will become more familiar with Gabriel as we continue through the book of Revelation.

We must understand the position of angels in the heavenly realm. There are different tiers of angelic power used by God. Some angels are identified as "mighty angels," others are called "special angels," and some as just angels. We should see that angels can be given enormous power over certain situations. Angels were there at the tomb opening of Christ to tell His followers that He had risen. All of those who know Christ as their Savior have been assigned angels to watch over them, (Psalm 91:11). In the Book of Revelation, we read about the activity of angels in almost every chapter.

NOW BACK TO OUR TEXT IN REVELATION

Read – Chapter 5:6

Who is worthy to open the seven seals? There was only One who had paid the price to break the seals on the scroll. The information that was contained in it would begin the time promised by God so very long ago. John wept deeply for a moment because no one was identified right away to be worthy to open the seals.

We see in this passage that one of the elders was capable of communicating with John, and that the elder interrupted in his worship of God long enough to console John. He told John to stop crying, as the Lion of the Tribe of Judah, the "Root of David," approached the Throne in which God was sitting. Only Jesus was qualified to open the seals of this scroll. After all, the first Fourteen Judgments on this world would be from Jesus Himself. The last seven bowls of pain are called the "Wrath of God" and are carried out by God the Father.

The conversation between John and the elder says to me that these elders had been with God for a very long time, some certainly well before the time of the ascension of Jesus. They understood what was happening in heaven and that there was a time coming when heaven would change and the family of God would be united. They were not just created beings without having independent thought that could only worship God.

Read – Chapter 5:7-9a

It had to be obvious to John that he was looking at the Son of God, the Lamb slain for the sin of this world. He was viewing the power of the Lord. He had seven horns, which would be to show the completeness of Christ, and His power displayed in the perfect number of seven. The seven spirits are sent out to the whole world through and by the orders of the Lamb. This is a great picture of Christ working with the seven angels and seven spirits of the church. As Jesus walked, so the seven spirits and seven angels walked with Him. These spirits are still in our churches today. Many of them have to be appalled at the behavior of the popular Christian church. There is no question that all of the occult religions are busy knocking on the doors of America trying to sell their rebellious position that attempts to challenge the authority of God.

What a perfect picture of our Savior and Lord as we read these verses. Who else could be considered to be worthy of opening the seals that would bring about the fate of this world? Only Jesus can accept the job of beginning the Tribulation Judgments. The people have been warned that this day was coming, and now it is here. Christ Jesus at once accepts the transfer of this information contained on the scroll, and all those around the throne worshiped the Lamb who was worthy to be worshiped, and worthy to open the seven seals.

An interesting note here in this text is that the elders are also musicians as they pick up harps and begin to play a new song for the Lamb. As the Elder's play their harps, the music blends in with the sweet smell of our prayers as incense going up to God. Millions of angels surround the Throne of God, recognizing the worthiness of God's Son. The angels smell the sweet incense of our prayers as they rise to the Lord for the needs of our church and our families and the honoring of the sacrifice that our Lord made on the cross

Read – Chapter 5:9b-10

Christ Jesus is the only One who is worthy to take the scroll. Who else in the world would be worthy to take on the task of ending this world with justice and fairness? Who else was destined to die for the sins of all mankind? It is sad to say that millions upon millions of people will reject the One who is able to take the scroll. Jesus has said that justice will be His and now He is about to serve as the Supreme Judge of the people in this world.

Acts 17:31...*For he has <u>set a day</u> when he will <u>judge the world</u> with justice by the man he has appointed. He has given proof of this to all men by raising him from the dead.*" History has proved His resurrection.

Read – Chapter 5:11-12

This is a moment when all the inhabitants of heaven come together to worship the Lamb of God. Heaven proclaims the worthiness of Christ Jesus to take on the responsibility of guiding us through the "End Time." Every angelic being and all those around the throne sing with one voice, with one message, and with a resounding approval and adoration of the Lamb who is worthy to receive all power and all glory. Jesus is described as having seven horns and seven eyes, (symbolizing power and authority). The text speaks of Jesus looking as if He had been slain; of course, His body would always show the manner in which those on earth treated Him.

It is important that we understand that all of this was settled before the earth was created. None of what people did in the past, no matter what will happen in the future, will be a surprise to the Godhead. I understand that this concept can be difficult to grasp, but when we read the Scriptures, pray, and then add faith in our daily lives, heaven will be revealed and we can see the intent of our heavenly Father. I know I have repeated this from an earlier paragraph, but I want you to understand what Christ will be doing for us in the end.

Read – Chapter 5:13-14

Of course, all of heaven recognizes Jesus for His mercy of coming to earth and making Salvation available to all the Gentiles of the world. Prior to His coming, only the Jewish people were destined to live with Christ for eternity, or that is what the prophets of old said. However, we read many references in the Old Testament about the Gentile Age and a time when the eyes and ears of God's favorite people would be closed to their Messiah. All of us should thank God that He makes it possible for us who are Gentiles to spend eternity with Him instead of eternity in hell (Isaiah 6:9).

Now we see the universe of God proclaiming the worthiness of Jesus to accept the position of the One who is to preside over eternity. The day has come that every knee will bow and every eye see the glory of God through the Son, Christ Jesus. When the days of sorrows are over, those of us who have accepted Him as our Lord will worship the Lamb of God forever.

PRELUDE TO THE JUDGMENTS

You are about to read about the judgments that will come upon this world. It is important to remember that there are two different judgments by two different Holy Beings. The first Judgments are from the Christ of God and the last judgment is the "Wrath" from God the Father. Jesus will bring judgment to the people of this world through what is known as "Seal Judgments" and "Trumpet Judgments." God the Father will bring about the "Bowl" or "Vial" Wrath. It is important to remember this because we will see that because of the split in judgments, two by Jesus against all people left on the earth when the Tribulation begins; and one Wrath of God against a society of those who refused to recognize God's Son, we will see this neutralizes any conversation about a Pre-Tribulation Rapture. I am not saying that all Believers will be left on earth to the extreme end of the Tribulation; no, there will be a "harvesting" of the saints of the Lord prior to the Wrath of God as He delivers the Bowl (Vial) judgments. (Revelation Chapter 14)

What you are about to read is the most exciting time in the history of man. Finally, Jesus will fulfill His promise to all those who are alive when He returns to take them home to be with Him forever. Those of us who have died earlier will come with Christ as He unites His entire family for the first time.

Joel 2:1-2a..._Blow the trumpet in Zion; sound the alarm on my holy hill. Let all who live in the land tremble, for the day of the LORD is coming. It is close at hand—a day of darkness and gloom._

CHAPTER 6

Six of the Seven Seals

PLEASE NOTE: We have been examining heaven and the Throne area of God with John. Now we are about to look at what will happen to the earth and its inhabitants as heaven opens and the Lamb of God takes physical control of His creation.

I should also note here that the earth has been through a time of worldwide chaos, which was eased by the antichrist. He will make peace treaties and will steal the hearts of the world. People will trust his judgment and decisions. Most will believe that he is sent from God as a god himself. Even many of the church will embrace him.

The punishment part of the Tribulation will begin the very moment the First Seal has been broken. Exactly when the Seal Judgments will happen as the Tribulation begins has been open to discussion. Many Believers believe it will happen at Mid-Tribulation. The Christian community must be able to identify the initiation of the Tribulation long before it starts. After identifying the beginning of the Birth Pains as explained to us by the "Great Teacher" in Matthew 24; we do not know how long these birth pains will last, nor are we given the precise time they will begin, but we can identify the pre-tribulation pain and suffering by these verses. We will quickly identify the hate and anger that will be prevalent in the beginning. As we begin to see our families disintegrate before our very eyes, along with the intensity of the persecution of the church, we should be able to identify these signs as the Tribulation nears. If we wait until we see the antichrist turn on Israel after three and a half years into the Tribulation, it will be too late for people to turn around and follow Christ. The pressure on the population of the earth will be tremendous, as the False Prophet demands that everyone worship an idol that mirrors the antichrist located in a wing of the Temple of God. If Christians cannot identify the "Birth Pains," they will be deceived and not find what they have been anticipating concerning eternity with their Lord. (Matthew 24:4-8)

The Book of Matthew reference above warns us to be careful of what religious leaders are saying. It has to be very confusing for any person who was not raised in any church to understand why there is such a huge variation between the doctrines of the churches. Here once again, we will hear of so-called prophets claiming equality with God and His Son Jesus. That is why it is so important to understand exactly how Jesus will return. He will come as described in Chapter 11:15-19 of Revelation.

We should also understand that all of the seals must be broken one at a time to open the scroll. Jesus will read the scroll containing the judgments at His timing. Each Seal judgment will play a significant role leading up to the unveiling of the end time events, including the "Trumpet Judgments." The Christ of God will deliver the first two Seal and Trumpet Judgments. The last Vial (bowl) Wrath will be directly from the hand of God the Father. It is a good idea to write down each of the Seal and Trumpet judgments listing them side by side. In doing that, you will see a pattern that could indicate to you that these judgments may overlap as the end of each judgment is given. You will see that because of the severity of each judgment, it may be possible that the final Two Judgments of Christ will be delivered at or near the same time the last Wraths of God are poured out on the world. All this pain and suffering of the first two Judgments by Christ is meant to bring people to Jesus. The Wrath of God is delivered to a society that has no hope of salvation and will be seeing the power of the God they rejected and mocked.

In Chapter 6, the Tribulation Period is just beginning. Let's read about what will happen before the end time events begin. The First Seal Judgment begins the Judgments of Christ. Earlier, I pointed out a time that Jesus called the "Birth Pains" mentioned by Him in Matthew,

Chapter 24. At this point, many Believers will be in jail for their beliefs and many will have been executed for their testimony for our Lord.

Nothing can be turned around at this point. The only thing that man can do now is to recognize Christ Jesus for who He is, and accept Him as their Savior and Lord. All of those things we read about in the Gospels about many turning away from Christ, and the love of most growing cold have already happened.

Can you see this happening right now in our world? Christianity is being attacked throughout the globe. Even those who once stood beside us in conflicts all over the earth are now putting a distance between themselves and us. The United States is even more fractured within itself than it is with old allies. The lack of respect and awe for God has left this country and we are now at the mercy of those who lead us.

At this moment in time, there have been several countries overthrown by the citizens of their respective nations. These countries surround the nation of Israel. Most of the men who have been overthrown or killed had a reputation of being tyrants. We would normally be happy to see them go. However, as we look at the results, we see factional governments taking over the countries. We can see the prophecy for or about the Last Days fulfilling itself right before our eyes.

As you read this, you will see that most of the things spoken about in this section of Matthew 24 do not take place during the Tribulation, but are events that will happen to Believers before the Judgments we are about to read. There is no disclaimer in this text saying that Believers in the United States will be immune from persecution, hatred, and being put to death for their beliefs. We here in the United States will suffer along with others throughout the world for our beliefs. As we look around us now, we see the devastation caused by radical Islamic militants here in our own country.

History will show that toleration of sin and evil will be the downfall of our country. We have already experienced death to the Christian community and others when the "Twin Towers" in New York City were attacked. The evil factions of this world have declared a war. War that is declared by using the name of God as a reason for the death of millions is monstrous. The Creator of this world will bring about an unspeakable carnage upon those who refused to honor His name. We have become so tolerant in this country that we actually considered allowing an image of those who killed our countrymen disguised as a place of worship within a block of the Twin Towers devastation. Who would have ever believed such a thing would happen in a God fearing nation? Now, we here in the United States are debating whether we should invoke some parts of Islamic law. I would like to say that there is a glimmer of hope that we here in the United States would stand up and insist that our nation return to its original values established by our forefathers, but the Bible says that the next great leader to come upon the scene internationally will be the antichrist. You know that other countries that hate us have infiltrated our borders. We must be careful that we do not maintain a mind set that all people from foreign nations are here to destroy us, but we must be vigilant. It is my prayer that many people who have come here to hurt this country find the God of the Scriptures and turn their life over to a loving and peaceful God.

First Seal Judgment

Read Verses 1-2

We find out that all four of these creatures in the Throne Room can communicate with John. The first creature showed John a rider on a white horse looking like a conqueror. He had a bow in his hand and a crown on his head. We know that this is not Satan because He has been, and is roaming the world, trying to steal away the Believers of Christ. He will soon give his authority over to the antichrist. This was the history made by God and now it was time to reveal such history as the first of the Four Horsemen of the Apocalypse is released. He is a rider bent on conquest, but he is lacking in several areas. First, there is no mention of the arrows for the bow. If he were to gain power over the world, it would have to be in the political arena. Second, the crown he has is not described as a crown of a conqueror. He rides to earth thinking he is a conqueror, but it is only another counterfeit thought in his own mind. He wants to conquer and shows all the signs of a conquering hero, by performing miracles, but he is a counterfeit. He is given the symbols of power, i.e. a white horse, a crown, and political savvy (the bow), but he lacks the power needed to conquer the earth. It is my feeling that this horse carries the evil Beast, the antichrist. Prior to this event, Satan roamed about the earth trying to pollute the minds of Believers and draw them away from their faith. This rider being introduced now believes he is the christ of Satan, the one who will challenge the God of heaven for ultimate authority. The counterfeit godhead will press hard now to draw away the church from God. The antichrist will try to erect a wall between those who are strong Believers and can overcome his evil, and the church that is weak and will not be able to stand against him. Many Believers will implode with doubt and fear leaving the safety of Jesus. They will follow a man who has taken on a god image and will prove his powers by performing miracles.

Over the years, many have fostered various theories such as the Pre-Tribulation Rapture that will lead many to abandon Christ when the rapture does not happen and they are left to rely totally on Christ Jesus. It will be a terrible day for the church and those who have misled the body of Believers. Now, if you are reading this today (2013), you probably will not go through the Tribulation period. However, there is a good chance that our children, grandchildren, and great grandchildren could experience what we are talking about right now. I say this to warn you that it is important to explain to our children that they may not be rescued through any supposition concerning the "catching up" of the church of Christ near or at the beginning of the Great Tribulation.

If it is true that there will be Pre-tribulation Rapture, there will be no harm in reading this material. If we are correct about what the Bible is saying, your family will be saved from seeking out a savior that may indeed be the antichrist and be duped into following him. We understand that Christ will come with His angels in the clouds to harvest His church, that church will return to earth with Him in what the text calls the "Second Coming of Christ," to erase all sin from the earth. It will be a noisy affair and the entire world's population, including those who ran the spear into His side as He hung on the cross, will see Him in all His glory.

Matthew 24:30-31…*"At that time the sign of the Son of Man will appear in the sky, and all the nations of the earth will mourn. They will see the Son of Man coming on the clouds of the sky, with power and great glory.*

And he will send his angels with a loud trumpet call, and they will gather his elect from the four winds, from one end of the heavens to the other.

Related Verse(s) / Revelation 1:7...*Look, he is coming with the clouds, and every eye will see him, even those who pierced him; and all the peoples of the earth will mourn because of him. So shall it be! Amen.*

It is painfully clear that we who believe in Christ Jesus, and are still on this earth at the beginning of the Tribulation, will see the antichrist take over the world with his power. What John is seeing now are the events that have been prophesied by the prophets of the Old Testament. The evil that exists right now was spoken about hundreds of years ago.

With the opening of the seals, a new era of chaos begins to envelop the world. This coincides with the timing of the Tribulation period when after three and a half years the antichrist breaks a peace treaty he brokered with Israel and sets up an image of himself for the world to worship.

Daniel 7:25...*He (antichrist) will speak against the Most High and oppress his saints and try to change the set times and the laws. The saints (Believers) will be handed over to him for a time, times and half a time. (3 ½ years)*

Daniel 9:27...*He will confirm a covenant with many for one 'seven.' In the middle of the seven he will put an end to sacrifice and offering. And on a wing of the temple he will set up an abomination that causes desolation, until the end that is decreed is poured out on him."*

Read – Chapter 6:3-4

Second Seal Judgment

Here again we are told of another creature that speaks to John. How are we to look at this fiery red horse? This sounds like the third member of the counterfeit godhead of the evil world. The False Prophet will indeed have the power to take peace away from the world. He is the perfect person to do this. The False Prophet will also demand that everyone take the Mark of the Beast. Peace will be taken from the nations of the world, and the hatefulness of men will increase beyond measure.

As the antichrist gives more power to the False Prophet, he will step up his efforts to renew chaos into the world's economy. The man will appear as one who knows all and is all-powerful as he demonstrates his power with miracles and wonders.

As quickly as the antichrist establishes worldwide peace, that peace will be stripped away. Only one thing will matter to the antichrist after the peace treaty with Israel is withdrawn, and that thing is the destruction of the church of God. Some of the church cannot fathom the idea that they would have to suffer at all. Most of the churches that feel this way are located in the United States. They feel that God will not ask them to stand against evil, but will reward their cowardice by taking them away from any danger.

The False Prophet will introduce the "Mark of the Beast." We have had some experience of a mark or a scar left by a microchip in our animals and in some cases our children. This sounds like a great idea, at first, but let's look at the consequences of this plan. The Mark of the Beast will mean that you are accepting a one world monetary system. The Mark of the Beast will replace any cash money system. People will shop and pay by passing their hand or body through a scanner that will automatically take the money from their account. The sad part about this mark is that those who take the mark will not be able to enter heaven to be with the Lord.

If you are a Believer, you will give up your place in heaven. Later we will read about one third of the church losing what they thought was a place in heaven because someone told them they would not have to enter the Tribulation period, and they gave their position up by taking the Mark of the Beast. The Bible plainly shows that any such theory is a hoax and it is very disturbing to see the church in so much confusion. (Revelation 13:16-17)

The message to stand firm until the end will be the key for the saints during this time. It will be extremely difficult. We will watch some of our brothers, sisters, fathers, and mothers turn against us. There will be a level of hate for the children of God that will exceed anything we have seen to date. The church will be caught up in the power of the antichrist and his prophet. The Mark of the Beast will be seen as a good thing. Without using money there will be no more street dealers of drugs, bank robberies will be halted, and no money schemes will be conjured up to steal money from the people. The same will be true of those Believers who will be prevented from doing any business because they have refused the Mark. Many people will take the "mark" without giving it a thought, and once that mark has been taken, it will not be able to be erased. We MUST be vigilant as the time nears when the church will be challenged severely. (Revelation 14:9-10)

Third Seal Judgment

Read – Chapter 6:5-6

A fair day's wages for a fair day's work is a thing of the past when this rider appears on earth. This will be a devastating event for all people. No matter how hard men will work at this time, they will only make just enough to survive each day. In other words, the economic structure of the world will be obliterated.

The government will pass out only the money needed for each family to keep from starving. The local governments will hold a majority of jobs. The government I am speaking of is the world authority. Elected local governments will be abolished and replaced by a world authority. A World Bank and government offices will have sub-offices throughout the world. We will see the effects of the first rider's political devastation. Famines will dominate the world. Hunger will turn the world into a place of hate and anger. The burning of the acid in men's stomachs will override the senses of charity and love. Love will grow cold as ice and the world will start preparing for a final battle. Look what is happening in our country today (USA). The economy is in the tank, and quite frankly the future looks very dim. We can imagine a time of restoration and financial things brought back to normal, but that is not in the nature of man. As the leaders of the world's economy look at each other for answers, each one seems impotent to solve the problem. They will be looking for one man to solve these problems. When the man (the antichrist) comes along, he will be accepted quickly as the one who will restore the world's economy again.

Read – Chapter 6:7-8

Fourth Seal Judgment

There are two riders on this horse. The first is death and the second one is Hades. Although this part of Scripture takes up little space the destruction as a result of this Fourth Seal would take the lives of at least one fourth of population, it was a gruesome affair. This world has known many plagues over the years. It is one of the most painful ways to die and oftentimes it takes many weeks, even months, for the patient to expire. As we look at death by the sword we can imagine what that must be like as the victim can die a lonely slow death by bleeding or the death can be quick as the sword passes through the neck and takes the head of the victim off his body.

Another method described for us is death by hunger. We have all seen pictures in the newspaper or on television that shows us the bodies of those who have gone without enough nourishment to survive. Along the way to their death many other body functions begin to stop functioning and death slowly devourers the targeted person or persons.

The last method of the death sentence being handed out by God for one-quarter of the earth is to be killed by wild beasts. All of this verifies the words of God as He says there is no place to hide from Him who has watched the world spit on His Son. This Son came to earth to give every man and woman a chance to have their sins forgiven and to guarantee them eternal life on a New Earth under a New Heaven.

We have all been told about the Gospel of Christ Jesus. Many people of the world saw the miracles of Jesus as He walked the earth. Many false prophets have come along over the years with their own stories of their great power. Some of them actual said they were the Son of God, others said God sent them. However, not one single so-called prophet was able to mimic what Jesus did when He was on earth. During a time in the future, a man will come on the scene that will indeed perform many of the miracles Jesus did. Unfortunately, this man of evil will seduce many of those who are in the church.

<u>Words of Warning</u>

Related Verse(s) / <u>Revelation 1:18</u>...*I am the Living One; I was dead, and behold I am alive forever and ever! <u>And I hold the keys of death and Hades.</u>*

Related Verse(s) / <u>Revelation 14:11</u>...*And the smoke of their torment rises for ever and ever. There is <u>no rest</u> day or night for those who worship the beast and his image, or for <u>anyone who receives the mark of his name.</u>*"

•◦●▬▬▬▬▬◆▬▬▬▬▬●◦•

Read – Chapter 6:9-11

Fifth Seal Judgment

This section of verses recognizes those who have lost their lives because of their testimonies for Christ Jesus. The souls under the altar of God tell us that the church is under persecution at this time and these souls would have to wait until all those predestined to be killed for the Lord are put to death. These souls are obviously the ones who had lost their lives during the Tribulation, and were ready to serve their Lord for a thousand years. Be careful to look at the statement that Jesus makes in verse 11; *"Then each of them was given a white robe, and they were told to wait a little longer, until the number of their fellow servants and brothers who were to be killed as they had been was completed."* This statement says that the Tribulation is still in progress and that more Believers would be coming to the altar area. They are given whites robes and told to wait until their fellow brothers and sisters completed the plan of the Lord.

Related Verse(s) / <u>Revelation 7:13</u>...*Then one of the elders asked me, "These in white robes--who are they, and where did they come from?" I answered, "Sir, you know." And he said, "These are they who have <u>come out of the great tribulation</u>; they have washed their robes and made them white in the blood of the Lamb.*

This is as good a place as any to speak of the two places Believers; those who have been born-again, spend their time until the Harvesting of the Saints and Second Coming of Christ. The first place is the Paradise of God, where all Believers that die before the Tribulation period will stay. The second place for Believers who are killed in the

Tribulation will be the souls we read about under the altar of the Throne Room of God, waiting to rule with Christ for a thousand years during the Millennium. More souls will be added to those under the altar as the Tribulation continues. Some believe that the souls under the altar will be only those who have been beheaded during the Tribulation. Others believe that everyone who has been beheaded for the name of Christ, including those in the Old Testament will rule in the Millennium.

Those who died before the Tribulation are in Paradise with the Lord and with those who have gone ahead. That thousand-year wait for our reunion with our brothers and sisters will not be much of a factor as we wait throughout the Millennium. Remember, that all souls will live forever. We who are in the Paradise of God will not have a problem waiting for the Millennium to be over and then be re-united with our brothers and sisters. Those who have rejected Christ before the Millennium will be in a place called Hades. This place is similar to hell we hear about. Hades is a very hot place and extreme torture will be the order of the day. People often joke about getting together and playing poker or some other game in Hades. The problem is that this place is described as completely dark and filled with the sounds of horror. It will be a very uncomfortable place to live, but will be nothing compared to the second death. In the second death, all unsaved people will be tormented in the Lake of Burning Sulfur for eternity without any mercy. This happens after the one thousand year reign of Christ is over and the Great White Throne Judgment begins. Let's take a look at a story about a rich man who is in Hades right this very moment. A rich man who demonstrated a lack of compassion begs for His family to be warned of hell.

Related Verse(s) / Luke 16:20-24... *"There was a rich man who was dressed in purple and fine linen and lived in luxury every day. At his gate was laid a beggar named Lazarus, covered with sores and longing to eat what fell from the rich man's table. Even the dogs came and licked his sores. "The time came when the beggar died and the angels carried him to Abraham's side. The rich man also died and was buried. In hell, where he was in torment, he looked up and saw Abraham far away, with Lazarus by his side. So he called to him, 'Father Abraham, have pity on me and send Lazarus to dip the tip of his finger in water and cool my tongue, because I am in agony in this fire.'* Does this sound like a great place to be with your friends? This torment will last forever for all those who reject Jesus as their Savior. You would think that the majority of the people who heard this story would accept Jesus immediately just in case they die prematurely. I am not writing this book to scare you, but we MUST pay attention to what Christ is saying to all of us; if our name is not written in the Book of Life, we will end up in the Lake of Burning Sulfur forever! Revelation 20:11-15

Read – Chapter 6:12-17

Sixth Seal Judgment

This sixth seal that is broken will be as we near the end of the Tribulation period. I believe it will follow in sequence of late end time destruction. This seal will be a challenge for all Believers. I will follow up on this thought later as we near the final Wrath of God.

The next to the last seal begins with a worldwide earthquake. The sun will be covered by what looks like a heavy cloth. This will bring about a temperature drop that will be devastating. The moon will look like it is suffering from internal bleeding. The tides of the oceans will be erratic because of the physical changes of the moon. The stars will fall to the earth and the sky will be rolled up like a scroll. Now, of course we all know that if every star fell to earth there would be nothing left of this world. In fact, there are hundreds of stars larger than this earth.

So, we must look at what Christ is trying to tell us here. If you have seen recent pictures of serious earthquakes on television, you have noticed that there is a great deal of dust in the area because of the displaced earth. In the case of a total-world earthquake, the dust coming from the ground would be an event that would be hard to imagine. When trying to look up in the sky, those who experienced this would not be able to see the sun, and the dust would make the moon appear red. This earthquake moved mountains and islands from their positions. Please notice here that the mountains were not leveled, but moved. By the way, we are not given the number of people killed by this quake.

The result of this quake will drive kings as well as the poor into the caves in their countries. The living conditions will be so bad, the air will be hard to get into the lungs of those trying to breathe, and getting any oxygen out of the air will be barely possible. While these people will be hiding in the caves, instead of reaching out to the Lord for salvation, they will call upon the mountains to fall on them. Even though they will see the power of God repeatedly, and will be aware of the power that the "Throne Room of the God" represents, their hearts will be hardened and thus be subject to the second death for all who are rebellious.

NOTE: CHAPTER SEVEN HAS BEEN MOVED TO THE END OF CHAPTER FOURTEEN. YOU MAY CHOOSE TO GO THERE NOW, OR WAIT UNTIL IT FALLS IN LINE WITH THE CHRONOLOGY OF THE REVELATION OF CHRIST.

CHAPTER 8

Silence & Four Trumpets

Read – Chapter 8:1

Seventh Seal

*When he opened the **seventh seal**, there was*
silence in heaven for about half an hour.

In Chapter Six, we were taken ahead of time to the point where it seemed
that all judgments had been given and the old earth was destroyed.
However, we will find out what really happened in further chapters.
Up until this point the Throne Room was very active. The creatures,
elders, and angels have been demonstrating their love for God with loud
praises, songs, and shouts of praise for the King of Kings. Heaven has
never been a quiet place, but now we hear a deathly silence leading to
an expectation of the last days of the existence of the earth.

Now all of a sudden there is complete silence in heaven. This will
be a spine-chilling time for the spiritual world as well as the earthly
kingdom. We know that the evil spirit world is always attacking the
Holy Spirit and that there is a struggle everyday that goes on between
good and evil in each of our lives. Even Satan and his demons will be
shaken to the core to hear the lack of noise coming from heaven. I am
told that there is such a silence sometimes when hurricanes are passing

through an area. Once the initial damage has been experienced, there is a quiet eerie calm and even sunlight can appear for a moment; then the backside of the storm hits with even more power than the first surge. People who are aware of this tell of the intense fear and the awesome destruction that then takes place. So it will be with this time of silence. Evil knows its days are numbered and this silence begins the quick demise of the world and the evil it represents. If Satan and his followers have forgotten what this time would mean for them, the silence will stun them back to reality as the stillness reminds them of what their fate is in the end. Horrible torture and persecution await them in a place called the Lake of Burning Sulfur. They will join all those who have turned their backs on the Lord and rejected His love.

Read – Chapter 8:2-4

After the silence, seven angels appear before the throne. These angels stand ready to call out the Trumpet Judgments of the Savior on the godless people of the earth. The previous seal judgments brought about by Christ, one seal at a time, have exhausted the people. Soon they will experience the Wrath of God after the "Trumpet Judgments" are completed. Another angel appears with a censer. This censer is filled with the prayers of all the saints of the earth and it is mixed with incense as the prayers are offered to God. These prayers are sweet smelling to our Lord. He is about to answer all those prayers that have asked Him to come quickly and rescue His family. I hope you understand just how much the Lord wants to hear your prayers. They are a sign of obedience and respect to Him. How many of you grow weary of praying and thinking nothing is happening in heaven and that your prayers are going unnoticed? Oftentimes, our prayers are answered in many other forms that not only help us, but glorify the name of the Lord. Read this text again in a different light knowing that your prayers are a part of those that are spoken of here.

1 **Peter 1:6**...*In this you greatly rejoice, though now for a little while you may have had to suffer grief in all kinds of trials.*

You read of the love that God has for us. He knows the battles we have had or are now fighting. Through it all, Christ has been our advocate to God, approaching Him with our requests. Jesus, after all, lived here on earth and is a perfect mediator explaining to God the needs of His people. Do not quit asking God for the desires of your heart. He wants to grant your requests as you glorify the Father.

Read – Chapter 8:5-6

It is only fitting that the prayers of these Tribulation Saints be the beginning of "The End." The same censer (a vessel in which incense was burned) was filled with a fire that would start the Trumpet Judgments. This censer that was used to burn the incense of all our prayers was now being used to hurl fire upon the earth. We can take pleasure in the fact that the vehicle used for us to communicate with God would be used to punish those who have denied Christ and perhaps persecuted us while we were on this earth. We share in the punishment of evil that has oftentimes persecuted us. There is a reason why God has asked us not to inflict revenge on those who persecute us. He will revenge our honor more intensely than we can. An earthquake starts the Trumpet Judgments. This earthquake is from the Throne Room of God so we can imagine the intensity of this event. (Romans 12:19 & Hebrews 10:30-31)

Fire becomes a dominant punishment as we approach the first of the seven Trumpet Judgments. The picture we see is a sad one as people, even church members, are accepting the Mark of the Beast. All those allowing this to happen to their bodies will go to a special place of eternal fire that has been set aside for their ignorance and outright disobedience to God. These are not my words, but the words of Christ. I am speaking of the church that, after accepting Christ, turns to the antichrist as Jesus personified. This is a little prelude to the second death, which results in these people being thrown into the "Lake of Burning Sulfur!" Now Trumpet Judgments are given to the residents of the world as their punishment grows even worse.

Related Verse(s) / Revelation 14:9-12...*A third angel followed them and said in a loud voice: "If anyone worships the beast and his image and receives his mark on the forehead or on the hand, he, too, will drink of the wine of God's fury, which has been poured full strength into the cup of his wrath. He will be tormented with burning sulfur in the presence of the holy angels and of the Lamb. And the smoke of their torment rises for ever and ever. There is no rest day or night for those who worship the beast and his image, or for anyone who receives the mark of his name. This calls for* *patient* *endurance on the part of the saints* *who obey God's commandments and remain faithful to Jesus.*

Read – Chapter 8:7

First Trumpet

Further destruction of the earth was coming. No matter which third of the world was burned up, the result will be devastating. Vegetation provides us with needed clean air to breath and is a source of nourishment, not to mention just the beauty of the land. We cry over a few thousand acres of land being destroyed by fire, or the devastation being caused by the reduction of our rain forest by greedy timber companies. Can you imagine what the devastation of one-third of our world being burned up will cause? The annihilation of life could be at risk during this event as fires break out all over the world. The destruction by the hail will no doubt be massive, assuming that it falls in populated areas. By the way, the destruction by fire is described as happening to "one third of the earth." The judgment being brought about may not be like dividing the earth by thirds and then destroying one third as we might think. The devastation caused by this first trumpet judgment may be worldwide in a hit and miss pattern. We are not told that human life was a target of this judgment, and of course, there is one-third of this earth that is still without humans living in the land.

No one will be fighting these fires because of the life-threatening barrage of hail, fire, and blood. Was there enough warning for those left on earth? Of course there was. The Scriptures have been telling of these events of this day for centuries. The sad thing about this is that not everyone who experiences this will accept Christ, but there are many who will take Jesus up on His offer. Why do you think people will denounce Jesus even given the torture they are going through? Well of course, it has much to do with the mind-set of man who believes He is in control of his life and no one else has the right to tell him what to do. He forgets that Jesus knew him before he was formed in his mother's womb, and that Jesus has the final control of where man will spend eternity. It does not make a single bit of difference to them that Jesus created the world and has the authority to do as He wills with us and the world.

Related Verse(s) / Jeremiah 1:5a…*"Before I formed you in the womb I knew you, before you were born…*

Acts 2:18b-19… *I will pour out my Spirit in those days, and they will prophesy. I will <u>show wonders</u> in the heaven above and signs on the earth below, <u>blood</u> and <u>fire</u> and <u>billows of smoke</u>*

Read – Chapter 8:8-9

Second Trumpet

The result of this trumpet is what appears to be a mountain on fire thrown into the sea. The first two Trumpet Judgments have an element of fire to them. How many more will have this same factor of fire?

This catastrophic event hits the pocketbook of the world. A third of the seafood industry is destroyed in an instant. Billions of dollars worth of shipping vessels sink to the bottom of the sea. The loss of life in the affected seas results in thousands of deaths. Perhaps millions of people lose their lives. Cruise ships in these areas will sink without a chance of survival because the sea has turned into blood and people will drown quickly. The stench of the sea animals that will float on the surface of these waters will be overwhelming. This will be a horrible day for those who were earlier laughing at the power of God as one-third of the seas turn to blood and millions of people die.

Zephaniah 3:8…*Therefore wait for me," declares the LORD, "for the day I will stand up to testify. I have decided to assemble the nations, to gather the kingdoms and to pour out <u>my wrath on them</u>-- all my fierce anger. The whole world will be <u>consumed by the fire</u> of my jealous anger.*

Read – Chapter 8:10-11

Third Trumpet

This is one occasion when the force of a star hitting the world will not affect its axis. It will be a force, which will appear as if an atomic bomb was detonated. The force of this judgment of Christ will be catastrophic. This great star that will be falling from heaven will explode into smaller pieces and affect one-third of the world's fresh water. This "Wormwood" is an actual plant mainly found in Palestine that makes water bitter. It is not normally poisonous, but it is a symbol of sorrow and calamity. In this case, it will cause many to die.

One-third of all fresh water lakes will turn bitter. Many municipal water systems draw their water from fresh water lakes. People will have to drink water that is very bitter just to stay alive, but they are unaware that this polluted water will eventually kill them. You would think that after all of this, the whole world would bow down and worship the Lord of Lords. However, even after all of this, many of the people of the earth remain unrepentant.

As the third Trumpet Judgment begins, one-third of a heavenly fire has scorched the earth and then one-third of the seas have turned into blood. Now, by the word of Christ, one-third of all fresh water is contaminated. The people alive on earth must be asking each other, what is coming next. A star seen by everyone, will have hit the earth with an atomic force that turns one-third of the earth's waters unbearably bitter. Two thirds of the world has been made unlivable. How many people will pray for repentance of their sins after this? We would think that almost all who see these three events would accept Jesus quickly, but we do not hear the numbers that finally repent of their sins.

Related Verse(s): <u>2 Peter 3:10-12</u>...*But the day of the Lord will come like a thief. The heavens will disappear with a roar; the elements will be <u>destroyed by fire</u>, and <u>the earth and everything in it will be laid bare</u>. Since everything will be destroyed in this way, what kind of people ought you to be? You ought to live holy and godly lives as you look forward to the day of God and speed its coming. That day will bring about the <u>destruction of the heavens by fire</u>, and the elements will melt in the heat.*

Read – Chapter 8:12-13

Fourth Trumpet

This trumpet sounds and its results will immediately lower the temperature of the world to freezing conditions. Days will be much shorter and climates of warm countries will experience the weather of the most northern countries. Gone with this catastrophe will be the growing and harvesting of the world's fruit and vegetables. Food will become scarcer. Darkness always brings about uneasiness and fear. Many people will become severely depressed. Others will be frightened, but very few to the point where they will see the Light of the Christ of God. All it would take is a repentant heart with a few sincere words accepting Jesus for who He is, to assure a future life of peace and comfort. (Romans 10:9)

As bad as all this has been so far, worse is yet to come. An angel of heaven gives a verbal warning to those left on earth. Jesus still wants the world to have a relationship with Him, even in these darkest of days. The problem is that time is growing short, and now the days can be numbered to just a few before The End. I am sure you will agree with me that the earth at this point is in deep distress. On top of all this, an eagle appears flying high over the earth with a horrifying message. We can imagine that everyone's television is turned on to witness this unusual event. There on Fox News will be the picture of an eagle speaking to the world with a message that is terrifying. The eagle will say three words, "Woe!" "Woe!" "Woe!" What the eagle is saying is that if you thought the previous four judgments were bad; hold on, the next three "Trumpet Judgments" will bring devastation with results that will be unequaled in this world. I keep on looking for cries of "Mercy-Mercy'" but there are no words of sorrow from the population that is left for a time of horror.

CHAPTER 9

Trumpets Five & Six

<u>**Read – Chapter 9:1-6**</u>

<u>Fifth Trumpet</u>

Once again, the full force of the sun and the moon would be taken away from earth's population. You have read these verses and are no doubt shaken by the extreme torture that will be given to those who have the Mark of the Beast and those who still reject the power of Christ.

What is this mark of the seal of God? Anyone who has accepted the Christ of God as their Savior has been marked by God through the Holy Spirit. This mark will prevent us from experiencing many of the judgments of Christ.

<u>Related Verse(s)</u> / <u>Ephesians *1:13-14*</u>...*And you were sealed in Christ when you heard the word of truth, and accepted the gospel resulting in your salvation. Having believed, **<u>you were marked in him with a seal, the promised Holy Spirit,</u>** who is a deposit <u>guaranteeing</u> our inheritance until the redemption of those who are God's possession--to the praise of his glory.*

Large groups of Believers still miss the freedom that God brings to those belonging to Him. God has sealed us for His Son Jesus, and with a seal that gives us heavenly protection as we suffer many trials. As we go through our life as a Believer, our goal in all we do should be to glorify God.

In Mark 5:11-14, demons that were in a man who lived in a cave asked Jesus not to send them to the Abyss. They asked Jesus to send them into a herd of pigs that were feeding on the hillside. Jesus granted their request which resulted in the death of the pigs. Of course, this could allow them to enter someone or something else later. The Abyss is the home base and the heart of Satan himself. The Abyss is a massive hole in the earth that leads to the core of evil. Nothing good can come up from the Abyss. Soon, Satan will find himself there to wait for 1000 years to be heard from again. Soon after that, he will end up in the Lake of Burning Sulfur to join others who thought they were in control of their destiny, including the False Prophet and the Antichrist.

The Abyss is so large and so hot that the smoke from this pit darkened what was left of the sun and sky which had lost one-third of their light in an earlier trumpet judgment. Can you see the end of this world coming? It will not be long now before Christ Jesus will be coming to spend 1000 years ruling this underlined refreshed world.

What will come up out of the Abyss will be dreadful. Locusts that look like scorpions will come up out of the pit and have authority to torture people for five months. They will not be allowed to sting any of those who have the seal of God. The sting of these beasts will make people suffer for five months in such agony that they will wish for death, but death will escape them. Death will be so close that they may feel that they could reach out and touch it, but mercy will not be shown to those who were so disobedient that they would suffer torment beyond the norm, but still reject Jesus.

Related Verse(s) / Ephesians 1:12-14…*And you also were included in Christ when you heard the word of truth, the gospel of your salvation. Having believed, you were marked in him with a seal, the promised Holy Spirit, who is a deposit guaranteeing our inheritance until the redemption of those who are God's possession--to the praise of his glory.*

Read – Chapter 9:7-11

Some have suggested that these beasts appeared to look like our modern day helicopter, although they are described to look like a horse. They will have the face that appears to be like man. I don't believe that anything coming up out of the Abyss would appear to be built by human hands.

Please understand that John was describing these things the best he could given the era he came from. I think the wise thing to do here is not to put much time into trying to describe what we are seeing here, but to concentrate on what these beasts are about to do to people. In any event, the result of the creature's sting will cause untold and unimagined suffering. Now we can say that all people finally understood who God was and why they should bow down and worship their Creator, but that would be untrue. Most people still hardened their hearts.

There is a king over this Abyss and his name is Abaddon, which means destruction! This king of the Abyss takes his orders from Satan, the king of evil. The word Abaddon is a synonym for "the grave". The grave is a place where the dead are buried and a place for those that are doomed to destruction. We can also describe this place as Hades, the place where the unsaved will stay until they experience the second death which will result in an encounter finding themselves being thrown into the Lake of Burning Sulfur forever.

Can you see the seriousness of these events? How critical is it that we tell everyone around us of the events that will soon take place? I understand if you are thinking I will not be a part of this, but I assure you that down the line in your family, perhaps even your grandchildren may see this happen. Don't you think they should be warned of the impending doom? They may reject your story, but when these things begin to happen, they may remember grandpa or grandma's warning of coming events and turn their life over to the Savior of the world, Christ Jesus.

Now we should think, and rightfully so, that most people at this point will stop and see that rejecting Jesus has consequences. The first "woe" spoken by the eagle had passed, now it was time for the second "woe." Let's look at what Jesus had to say when using the term "woe." The following verses are located in the same chapter that the blessings to others are listed. There is a time coming when the woe of God will mean something and terrify anyone who will be expecting more disaster. Instant gratification has been the driving force for humanity from the Garden of Eden up until the date you are reading this commentary. A terrible anguish will fall upon man in the following "Woe."

Related Verse(s) / Luke 6:24-26... *"But **woe** to you who are rich, for you have already received your comfort. **Woe** to you who are well fed now,* *for you will go hungry. **Woe** to you who laugh now, for you will mourn and weep. **Woe** to you when all men speak well of you, for that is how their fathers treated the false prophets.*

Read – Chapter 9: 12-16

Sixth Trumpet

The sound of this trumpet means war! One-third of the population of earth will be killed during this event. The great Euphrates River seems to be the launching point of many of the judgments of God against mankind. It is interesting to note that the Euphrates River as it meets other headwaters is where the Garden of Eden is still located.

It is also important to start thinking about how much of the earth's population has been killed to this point. Remember that one-third of the earth was killed here and one-quarter was killed in the fourth seal of Christ. There are not a lot of people left for the balance of the Wrath of God. Although we read about one-third of the earth waters being turned to blood and another third into bitter water that can kill, some people will find a way to live through these things. Although it may appear to them that they have had some success, it will be short lived, as in the end, they go against the Christ of God.

Related Verse(s) / Revelation 9:16…*The number of the mounted troops was two hundred million. I heard their number.*

Read – Chapter 9:17-21

The three things that kill all this humanity are fire, smoke, and sulfur. This war will not be fought with bows and arrows, but will be fought by Christ with no retaliation from man, even with all the modern weapons available to them. When we look at what is available to the world in weaponry, this war will end in terrible losses for mankind. In the end, the Wrath of God will result in the total destruction of mankind by the One who created them.

A war that kills a third of mankind yet the rest of the world will still refuse to repent. When catastrophe strikes someone else, we stand by in sympathy, but only for a short time. We still fall back to our lifestyle and believe it cannot happen to us. The message that no one will escape the Wrath of God is lost on the last of the diehards who still believe they are in control of their lives.

Once again, we see fire being used in this next to the last Trumpet Judgment. There will be only one more Trumpet Judgment and that will end the total Judgments of Jesus the Christ.

CHAPTER 10

The Little Scroll

Here again, we are stopped to speak of an event that will challenge our understanding of Revelation. There will be a couple more references in the middle of the story of the Harvesting of the saints, and we will stop and learn all we can about the subject Christ Jesus is addressing.

Whenever we come up upon a section of Scripture that requires much prayer and understanding, we often hear several different interpretations of the same writings. The following Scripture meets this pattern.

Read – Chapter 10:1-4

We are confronted again with another "mighty angel." who looks intimidating and is an example of great power. The description of this mighty angel comes very close to other verses that describe Christ. We must make sure that we are not quick to identify Jesus without context. In this case we read the identification of an angel doing these things in verse one. If we take what is written literally, this is one huge, mighty angel. The rainbow above the head of this mighty angel reminds us of another rainbow that was given to all creation by God. The rainbow is a symbol of promise.

John must have been becoming a little more adapted to mighty things around him as he begins to record what the "seven thunders" are saying. Now here is a situation that we could speculate as to what was on the little scroll, but in these cases, it is wiser to file this in our memory banks and be content to wait until we see Jesus and the answers will be given to us. I wish I could tell you what the "seven thunders" were, but although the Scriptures use the word seven, meaning perfection, and thunders, always used as a form of punishment in the book of Revelation. We are told about thunder in Psalm 29:3-9, which may give us a hint of what Jesus, is saying here in this text. I cannot put these together without some supposition. I believe when these situations present themselves, we should not speculate and thus cause someone to believe a lie rather than the truth.

This angel is clothed with a cloud. We should be somewhat familiar with that description as we speak of the return of Christ. He too, will come to earth with His angels in the clouds. We will see our Savior as He comes in the clouds to receive those who are left on this earth that belong to Him, who will be harvested by His angels. It is important that we do not confuse this angel's coming in the clouds with the description of the harvesting angel mentioned in Revelation fourteen. Again, it is clear that it would be better if we did not know the information detailed on this little scroll. As we read on we see that although the scroll tastes good in the mouth, it is not so good in John's stomach. We know all about appearances and that they can be deceiving.

As the mighty angel opened his hand, he planted his feet on both the sea and dry ground. Normally we would interpret standing in the sea to mean a group of people. Whatever the message was on the little scroll, it was obviously for all creation. The message lay open in the hand of this angel. The judgments that the world is in the middle of at this time will now come at a quicker pace. At this point, we are preparing to hear the last and final Trumpet Judgment. "There will be no more delay," the mighty angel said. This is very exciting for the family of Christ. The end is near for them soon. Jesus will come in the clouds with His angels, and they will harvest the children of God. These special angels gathering the saints will conclude the church age.

Read – Chapter 10:5-6

It is important that we pay attention to the prophets of old who explain the events of end times. Many Old Testament prophets tell us of the events during the Tribulation. We are close to the end here and the Lord wants us to be alert and ready. Although we are focusing on New Testament prophecy about the Second Coming of Christ, we can learn much from Old Testament prophets. I will give more references throughout this study.

Amos 9:13-15...*"The days are coming," declares the LORD, "when the reaper will be overtaken by the plowman and the planter by the one treading grapes. New wine will drip from the mountains and flow from all the hills. I will bring back my exiled people Israel; they will rebuild the ruined cities and live in them. They will plant vineyards and drink their wine; they will make gardens and eat their fruit. I will plant Israel in their own land, <u>never again</u> to be uprooted from the land I have given them," says the LORD your God.*

The verses above give us a glance into what the Lord has planned for part of His family, the Jews. In many camps, the Jews are overlooked when it is time to put End Time events together. It is important that we listen to what the prophets have told us through the Scriptures. It takes time and many hours of reading to understand what the prophets had to say to us concerning the end of the world and how it fits into Jewish future prophecy.

Read – Chapter 10:7-11

This is like accepting the message of eternal life through Christ Jesus, and then seeing what events must happen to fulfill God's word of eternity for us. John was instructed to prophesy to others of what was soon to take place. It was a bittersweet message, one of spending eternity with Jesus combined with what a person may have to go through to receive it. Of course, not all Believers will go through the Tribulation. Millions of them have already gone to be with the Lord and are waiting for us in the Paradise of God. The angel speaks of taking a message to all nations, languages, and world leaders. They will be wise to accept what Jesus has to say to them through the voice of John.

Revelation 10:7 *But in the days when the seventh angel is about to sound his trumpet, the mystery of God will be accomplished, just as He announced to His servants the prophets.*

The verse above forecasts what we will be reading in just a few minutes as we read Chapter Eleven. The final and last trumpet will be sounded that signals the church it is time that they will be brought home by being harvested by the angels of the Lord as He meets them in the clouds.

CHAPTER 11

Two Eternal Witnesses

Read – Chapter 11:1-6

John measured the Temple of God, but we do not see the measurements in this chapter. What we are about to read is the second "woe" promised to the world just a few verses earlier. Two witnesses will appear and have the power from the Throne Room of God to do what they think necessary to bring people to their knees. The length of time the Gentiles have to accept Christ is the same time the witnesses will be in Jerusalem. Of course, these witnesses must come at or near the beginning of the Tribulation, because they will only have 42 months to share the Gospel. Most will run roughshod over the sacred Temple area and ignore their opportunity to be accepted into the family of the Lord. These two witnesses will no doubt have to kill many people because of their hatred of God and these witnesses as they proclaim the Gospel.

Who are these two men? Both of them have been before the Throne Room on a regular basis. The Bible refers to these two men as solid and faithful as two olive trees. Olive trees are noted for the symbol of peace and strength used as a gesture of reconciliation or friendship. The decree of these two men is the Gospel message that Christ Himself gave many times during His ministry. In this case, these two individuals represent the last offer of spending eternity with the Godhead in peace and glory. They also are described as the "two lampstands that stand before the Lord of the earth". Please remember the description of the lampstands in verse twenty of Chapter One. The lampstands described there were the seven churches Jesus was about to address. I believe these men will specifically address the church of Jesus the Christ on the earth at this time. Many of us have been concerned about our churches for some time. You have seen what is happening to our churches. The church needs to be awakened by the stark realization that time is growing very short.

There have been many theories of who these two men are, but the only thing we can say for sure is that they are representatives of the Throne Room of God. These men will represent God and preach the message of His Son Jesus, "repent," for the kingdom of God is dangerously near. The names of Moses and Elijah are often mentioned when speaking of the two witnesses, but we really have no idea who they are.

They will be prophesying on this earth for three and a half years, as the antichrist brokers a peace agreement with Israel's neighbors. Their ministry will end just before the Seventh Trumpet has been sounded. These are peace loving men with just one message of love for the people. The only time the people of this earth will see the devastating power of these two men will come when they are threatened with harm or death. These special men from God will do all they can to convince others in the world to accept their message. They can do whatever it takes to get their message of hope and love through to man. If they see that closing up the skies from rain will result in just one person coming to Christ, they will do that. All that they do has the blessing from God. It may be that some people will need to see their intent by being exposed to their water source turning into blood. Others will be struck with various plagues to show the sincerity of these two witnesses.

Now we see the evil of Satan masquerading as the god with authority to temporarily kill the two witnesses. The power of Satan will seem insurmountable, people will say that Satan can kill God if the wishes. But his power is shown for what it is, in that three and a half days later, the two witnesses come alive by the breath of Christ. Satan is shown for who he is, an evil presence in the form of a heavenly angel come to earth to rally an army to defeat God. We read about the fall of Satan earlier in the life of this evil one called Satan or the Devil. Isaiah writes of the fallen angel called Satan, which is recorded in the book of Isaiah,

Chapter 14:12-15. Is there any doubt in your mind that this will be a terrible time for the people of the earth who have rejected the Truth of God? All the plagues of heaven are available for these two witnesses to convince humanity that they must recognize Jesus as Christ and the Messiah of the chosen people. On top of this, the judgments will continue, and soon the Last Trumpet will be sounded, and then the world will experience the total Wrath of God.

Read – Chapter 11:7-10

When these witnesses have finished their assignment, the beast coming out of the Abyss will temporarily kill them. Burial will not be an option, as the people want to see these two men's bodies decompose before their very eyes. Peoples of all the earth will file by to mock them and spit upon them as a sign of their hatred toward the Gospel message told by these representatives of the Holy Father. For three and a half years, the majority of the people will turn away from God no matter what these two men could do to them. People will treat this as a holiday as if it were Christmas or a special birthday. They will give gifts to one another in thinking they have outlasted the torture of God, but just like the final White Throne Judgment, they will be shocked at what comes next. This will be a time of their final celebration.

The people will think that they have won the battle, but they soon will see that God is in control. That is a mirror image of what is happening today in the world minus the two men. People will have this time to accept Christ, but they will laugh in the street and spit on those who follow Him. The behavior of these people is reprehensive and representative of the evil nature that is in all of us. Part of this evil human nature comes out in a "mob mentality" and will rear its ugly head during this time. People who normally do not get involved in such evil will be willing participants in an evil rebellion without conscience. The only assurance of not participating is to be a son or daughter of Christ Jesus.

Read – Chapter 11:11-14

What a shock! These men of God came to life after three and a half days. God breathed air into the lungs of these two prophets. The population of the earth had the opportunity of seeing the two prophets being gathered back to God in a cloud, just as Jesus went to be with His Father after the resurrection. If these two men could do so much damage while standing on earth, what will God do from the Throne Room? All of a sudden, flashes of warnings had to go through the minds of those who had been told about the Salvation of Christ by the Two Witnesses. Then, like in Old Testament times, a voice comes out of heaven saying, "Come up here." That phrase had to stop the hearts of those who heard the voice of God.

On top of the resurrection of these two men came a severe earthquake causing a tenth of the city to collapse. With seven thousand people being killed, the people gave glory to God because they were terrified. Here we read that at the end of this event, the people gave glory to God, but notice that they did not accept His Son as their Savior. They acknowledged that He was indeed God and capable of causing the destruction of their city. The lesson here is that acknowledging God is not good enough to be in the family of Christ.

Related Verse(s) / James 2:19... *You believe that there is one God. Good! Even the demons believe that--and shudder.*

THE LAST TRUMPET

Read – Chapter 11:15-19

The second Woe is over and now we shall see the third Woe that will bring down everyone whose name is not written in the Lamb's Book of Life. Now we're seeing through the words of John an event that was prophesied so many years before; that we would be hearing the blast of the last Trumpet, and what that would trigger concerning the Church of Christ.

Related Verse(s) / I Corinthians 15:51-52...*Listen, I tell you a mystery: We will not all sleep, but we will all be changed-- in a flash, in the twinkling of an eye, at the last trumpet. For the trumpet will sound, the dead will be raised imperishable, and we will be changed.*

The last Trumpet Judgment will signal the time for accepting Christ has passed. God will deliver His Wrath on earth shortly after the last trumpet sounds as Jesus meets His church in the clouds just before the seven final bowl/vial Wraths are given. The church will see the day it has looked for since the resurrection of Christ Jesus.

Heaven will be exposed for all to see the Throne Room of God. In clear view, the Ark of the Covenant will shine like the representative of God's power and design. Once again heaven will become a noisy place with lightning, rumblings and peals of thunder. On top of this will come an earthquake combined with a huge hailstorm. Would not all the people confess that He is Lord and ask Him to forgive them? Unfortunately, people still turn their backs on the only God offering eternal life in heaven.

Now the time is coming for judgment for both the good and the bad. The earth is done being a doormat for an ungrateful human race. A reclaimed earth will be given for 1000 years to the Christ of God and those who followed Him through the Tribulation by losing their lives, along with most of the chosen family of God, the Jews.

THE SEVENTH AND LAST TRUMPET SOUNDS

Immediately the noise level in heaven is increased. Voices will be saying that once again the world has become the sovereignty of the Christ of God. There will be no end of this reign, as it will last for eternity. We too will be part of that family of God that will see the benefits of knowing Jesus as our Lord and Savior.

Now we see the final judgment when Jesus will reward those who have followed His commands and lived their lives as Believers. As ALL of us will gaze at the Throne Room of the Godhead, we will see the Ark of the Covenant as lightning and thunder will come from heaven. All of this will bring about an earthquake and an enormous hailstorm. Now, preparation has to be made for a final battle between good and evil.

All the Believers left on earth before the final trumpet sounds will be in heaven after it has been blown. We will be there until after the Wrath of God is delivered to an unrepentant world. We will read about our mode of travel in Chapter 14 as it describes the Harvesting event.

Those who were Believers during the Judgments of Christ are brought to the Lord. Jesus will gladly accept us into His kingdom and the glory of His Father will shine.

The elders fell on their faces before the Lord. From this moment on, we hear the elders speak of the Wrath of God that has come and the eventual judgment that would send those who rejected Jesus to the second death of spending eternity in the Lake of Burning Sulfur.

NOTE: The next two chapters contain several events that are written in a form that may confuse you. Do not let that happen. Read them slowly and often if you are having a hard time putting things together. I pray that I have expanded on these events enough so that you will understand what is happening. Of course all questions can be sent to me by mail or e-mail.

Between The Chapters

Read This Before Continuing

Before going on to Chapter 12, I must stop here and explain what will be happening for the next few chapters. As you have read in Chapter 11:15-19, the final Trumpet Judgment was sounded and the church of Christ was gathered to their Savior by His angels as He was in the clouds. This is a fulfillment of several verses of Scripture, one being Matthew 13:39b, *"The Harvest is the end of the age, and the harvesters are angels."* and another one quoted in I Thessalonians 4:17, *"After that, we who are still alive and are left will be caught up together with them in the clouds to meet the Lord in the air. And so we will be with the Lord forever."* We also read about meeting Christ in the clouds in Mark 13:26.

Please note here that Jesus did not come to earth at this time, but He meets His church in the clouds and not on the streets of this world.

The next few chapters will tell us more of what was going on during the part of the Tribulation that directly affected the church of Christ. Many people get confused at this point and get lost in what Jesus is trying to tell us in the chapters ahead. This type of writing happened in the first three chapters of Genesis. The first chapter of Genesis told us about how God created the earth and the creation of the people on that earth. The second chapter of Genesis tells us of the particulars of that creation. Answers to questions like: What was God's intent when He created man and woman? When was Eve created? How did they feel?

How did they react to the only restriction they while in the Garden of Eden? What were they like? Did God create other men and women on the sixth day?

In the book of Revelation, we have just read the foundational chapters which introduce us to the Throne Room of God and how Jesus was going to fulfill His word to us by giving the answers to the questions that His Disciples had for Him while speaking of His death, resurrection, and the eternal life with the Godhead. We have just finished reading in the last chapter about the Harvesting of the Saints before God would deliver His "Wraths" upon an ungrateful people. He promised us that the Tribulation would be cut short for those who would believe and live for Him. Up to this point in our reading (Chapters 4-11), He has made His word good as we are now, at this point, in heaven to be with Him forever and will return to earth with Him at His Second Coming.

Beginning in Chapter 4, Jesus tells of the coming Tribulation and that we need to prepare for what is going to happen. He speaks of the Judgments of Christ, which are the "Seal and Trumpet Judgments." During this explanation, He stops from time to time to fill us in about other subjects that will fit into the final picture of the "End Times."

Once we get to Chapter 11, we are told of the Harvesting of the Saints. This time is often confused as the Second Coming of Christ. However, this is not the Second Coming of Christ; but a time that has been set aside to take His church home and keep them from the "Hour of Trial" (see Revelation 3:10 - the Wrath of God). What we read about in the next 7 chapters will be a deeper explanation of the events during the Great Tribulation period. As you read these chapters you will be able to understand better the seven years of Tribulation and how to be a better servant in spreading the Gospel and the truth about the coming of Christ for His church.

The Second Coming of Christ is explained in Chapter 19:11-21. There we will see Christ coming with His church to mark the end of this world. Those of us who have gone to the Paradise of God will spend the next 1000 years there enjoying our new eternal life. While we are in Paradise, the saints who have been under the altar of God will begin to rule with Christ in the Millennium. After those thousand years are over, we will join our family coming from the Millennium period and enjoy eternity with them on a New Earth and a New Heaven.

I hope this intermission in our text has helped you to understand the future. No one knows better than me the trouble of reading Revelation with so many theories out there, and the prophecy of false prophets who, for personal gain, have distorted the Word so badly. For those of you who see this subject of the end of the world to be an extremely critical time for Believers, I encourage you to share your experience of reading this commentary with your family and friends.

Special Events

Looking Back

CHAPTER 7

144,000 Jews Sealed

Read – Chapter 7:1-4

As I mentioned in the beginning of this Bible study, Revelation is not written in chronological order. There are times that John will stop and show us an event that is not in sequence with what was being shown to him by an angel, or Christ. This is one of those times. Moving this chapter to this location does not change the message of Christ whatsoever. Because this is a Bible study program, it is important to describe events separately that went on during the Tribulation phase. John was being shown a remnant of the Jewish population that will receive a special assignment to be near Christ for eternity. As we look at this group, we see that wherever Jesus goes, these men follow Him. Some say this group of Jews will be present during the Tribulation to spread the Gospel, but further reading in the Bible will debunk such an idea.

We must look at the reasoning for people thinking these Jews were to be used for spreading the Gospel. Those who believe this theory use the process of elimination as the basis for their thought. If the church is being caught up to be with the Lord before the Tribulation begins, who will tell those left on earth about the Gospel of Christ? We cannot just come up with a teaching like this and convince people of the idea without Scripture to back it up. Jesus, when asked to describe His Second Coming, said nothing concerning a rapture of the church before the Tribulation. He did however, tell us of a time when the church in total will be brought home to be with Him. This time is referred to as the "Harvesting of the Saints." We will study this in detail very shortly.

There is not one verse that has Jesus saying He will gather His church before the Tribulation. He does speak about the "birth pains" before the Tribulation begins and this would be one of many places in Revelation to tell of the rapture of the church. However, Jesus is silent on this issue until we come to the end of Chapter 11 and the middle of Chapter fourteen. You will see the story of the love Jesus has for His church and the promise to shorten the Tribulation for His Believers. The Scripture has to be twisted, convoluted, and broken into parts to come up with such a story as a Pre-Tribulation Rapture. Even then, it is obvious that people are reaching for a fairy tale ending of the world for the body of Believers. The Coming of Christ for His church at the appointed time just isn't wondrous enough for some people. They have to make up stories proclaiming they are so special that they will be taken out before persecution begins. Jesus said "if they persecuted me they will persecute you." See John 15:20 & Luke 21:12 for confirmation concerning who will be persecuted.

A great disaster is about to begin. Four angels are ready to hold back all the winds of the earth. Because the wind will be held back, an adverse effect on plant life, animals, and humans will result. John was looking at the time near the end of the Tribulation. This is important because we see this special group of Jews being introduced to us as they were in the presence of Jesus in heaven. These men were not on the earth, but they were in heaven to be with Jesus forever.

One hundred and forty four thousand Jews were to receive the Mark of God. A further explanation of the one hundred and forty four thousand is found in verses 2-4 of this Chapter. We see here that this group of Jewish men will receive a seal on their foreheads. This seal will prevent any judgment or wrath from affecting them. The first question that arises out of this is why do these men have to be protected since they will be with God continually? The answer is that Jesus will be in positions that have an element of sin within them, not to mention the Millennium covenant period. We will read more about this in the chapter on the Millennium.

After explaining who this group of Jews was, John immediately saw the Throne Room of God. We see here that all of the saints who were killed in the Tribulation stood in white before the Throne. The Tribulation was finally over.

I am sure you can understand why this particular event sandwiched between the sixth seal and the seventh seal could be confusing. If you will look at this as a time after the Tribulation has ended, it will make better sense to you. As I said earlier, the message is the same, but reading it now makes the chapter easier to place within the events of the Tribulation.

What was the group of Jews to do from this point forward? They were to serve Christ! They were perfect examples of how the Jewish nation should have accepted their Messiah. This section of the Revelation of Christ Jesus was inserted in this spot to identify exactly who these men were and how they will fit into the prophecy concerning the Christ of God.

Read – Chapter 7:5-8

Reuben 12,000,	*Gad 12,000,*
Naphtali 12,000,	*Manasseh 12,000*
Asher 12,000,	*Simeon 12,000,*
Issachar 12,000,	*Levi 12,000,*
Zebulun 12,000,	*Joseph 12,000,*
Benjamin 12,000	*Judah 12,000*

Notice that the Tribe of Joseph has replaced the Tribe of Dan. There is some speculation that the Tribe of Dan was omitted because of their outright disobedience in worshiping idols and blaspheming the Holy name of God. Proof is in the Scriptures below. I cannot stress enough the importance of realizing that when Christ says something will happen, you can count on it!

Related Verse(s) / Judges 18:30,31…*There the Danites set up for themselves the idols, and Jonathan son of Gershom, the son of Moses, and his sons were priests for the tribe of Dan until the time of the captivity of the land. They continued to use the idols Micah had made, all the time the house of God was in Shiloh.*

I Kings 12:28-30…*After seeking advice, the king made two golden calves. He said to the people, "It is too much for you to go up to Jerusalem. Here are your gods, O Israel, who brought you up out of Egypt. One He set up in Bethel, the other in Dan. And this thing became a sin; the people went even as far as Dan to worship the one there.*

This is a perfect example of what can happen to people who start out being spiritual, but then abandon their faith for the world's morals and evil standards. We have the same problems today with false gods and false prophets. All we need to do is look at how many gods people are worshiping in the various religions we have on earth.

Read – Chapter 7:9-10

Now look at the number of the great multitude, so many that John could not count them all. Notice that these people were from every nation of the world. It is obvious that we are seeing the end of the Tribulation and those who are with Christ at the end. These folks had heavenly bodies and wore white robes while they held palm branches in their hands. John looks way ahead in time, at a time when all who belong to Christ have left this earth and are rejoicing with the Lord. What a great time we will be having soon as we get ready to stand up for Jesus and wait for His return for us.

Don't be fooled by those who have appeared and have twisted the word of God to fill their pocketbooks and selfish ambitions. We have seen them in our recent past, haven't we? Look at the Jim Jones crowd in Ghana; they looked to their leader and rejected the words of God in the Bible. They took the fatal step in placing their faith in the words of a man who twisted the words of God and ended their lives by suicide. Other men like Thomas Ice, Tim LaHaye, and Hal Lindsay, although no doubt are not evil men, and filled with zeal, have mislead the average Believer by spreading a theory begun by a little Scottish girl in the early 1800's. These men may have good intentions, but they have lured millions of Christians into believing a false prophecy. These men come across as wise and all knowing and have gathered many into their false theory which will result in those who follow them to be sentenced to the "second death." Their theory is that Christ will sneak back to the world and take His church home before the Tribulation begins. Other antichrists have shown up in cults throughout the United States and the world. Jesus did not come to give us words that require theologians to put together for us. His message is simple and meant to confound the wise, and what we see in most commentaries about the end of time are stories by the so-called wise men of Christianity.

I pastor a church that is in the middle of a county in Virginia that is being populated by "New Age" followers from the Washington, D.C. area. We have large groups that have their base in transcendental meditation. Others are always trying to get in touch with the god within them, but deny the Most Holy God of Creation. Still others believe that they are some type of god and he/she is equal to the God of heaven. Pre-Tribulation people believe that Jesus will spare His church the terrible persecution of any part of the Tribulation. That thought will result in millions of Believers to believe in a false god who appears to be the Son of God, but is a liar.

The Jewish people are the chosen people of God our Father. God has given His Son Jesus to us through His death on the cross. Now is a time, during this church age, that we who are Gentiles are given the opportunity to be grafted into the Tree of Life, making us adopted Jews. We are fast approaching the time that the church age will be finished. It will happen at the time set forth by the writings in the Revelation of Christ, which you are studying now.

Romans 11:17-18 explains what it means to be grafted into the eternal life plan of Christ Jesus. You only have this opportunity during your life cycle, which can be short or long. Please do not let others sway your opinion about your life and how to live it. I am giving you an outline to read about what you personally will be responsible for as your life ends. I have not written this book to convince you about my message from the words of Christ, but I am asking you to read for yourself what God wants you to accept or reject. Reading the Bible critically will be an exercise that will change your life. Do not miss this opportunity to reach deeply into the heart of God.

We know that man is born into evil. If left to himself, he will turn within himself and hurt anyone who threatens him. We only need to look at Satan who elected to rid himself of the presence of God. We need God and we should count it all good to be grafted into His family, and should never be ashamed to be called an adopted Jew in the family of

Christ. Never forget that all the power of God is available to us through Christ Jesus.

Read – Chapter 7:11-17

We know by this Scripture that those involved in war will not see war again. The CHURCH AGE HAS ENDED long before this. Jesus will teach people how to follow Him through the Millennium. As we read this I am led to think about all the Christians who have gone on before us spending their time in the Paradise of God while the things on earth carry on to its end. The Millennium will include only those who have lost their life for Christ during the Tribulation. We should all agree that each one who lost their life should be rewarded with a special time with our Messiah. We who are in the Paradise of God will not be jealous of those who are reaping a reward for their service to the Savior. One of the wonderful things about eternity with Christ is that there will be no jealousy, hate, envy, gossip, backbiting, or pain as we live with the Lord forever.

These verses confirm the Tribulation is over. We do read a sort of strange conversation in verse 14; where the elder from heaven asked John where the people with the white robes came from. John answered saying they were they who had come out of the great Tribulation.

We are now going to read about the nation of people who will be in the Millennium. It is my opinion that the Jewish Nation will be translated to the Millennium world where they will be spending 1,000 years with their Messiah and have judges over them from the men who have overcome during the Tribulation. All those who lost their life for Jesus will be part of the heavenly court of God.

Here we read the prophet Isaiah as he refers to the people of the Millennium as they go in and out worshiping Christ and settling disputes. This is immediately after the Second Coming of Christ after the Wrath of God is over and Father God says, "It is over." There will be a 1,000-year reign of Christ with those who were killed in the name of Jesus. After the 1,000 years is over, Satan will be released for a short time from the Abyss, only to be defeated by Jesus and then thrown into the Lake of Burning Sulfur.

Isaiah 2:2-5…*In the last days, the mountain of the LORD's temple will be established as chief among the mountains; it will be raised above* *the hills, and all nations will stream to it. Many peoples will come and say, "Come, let us go up to the <u>mountain of the LORD</u>, to the house of the God of Jacob. He <u>will teach us his ways</u>, so that we may walk in his paths." <u>The law will go out from Zion</u>, the <u>word of the LORD from Jerusalem</u>. He will judge between the nations and will settle disputes for many peoples. They will beat their swords into plowshares and their spears into pruning hooks. Nation will not take up sword against nation, nor will they train for <u>war anymore</u>. Come, O house of Jacob, let us walk in the light of the LORD.*

We must remember that the people going into the Millennium to rule with Christ are those who were killed during the Tribulation. Another society will be alive during the Tribulation. Actually, there will be several different groups of people. We know this because those given the opportunity to serve as judges during the Millennium will need to have people to lead. I feel certain that the Jewish nation will be the one nation referred to in the Millennium. Of course, the Jewish nation is made up of twelve tribes and those tribes are sometimes referred to as nations. There will be no more fighting during the Millennium, but there still will be disputes during this time. Rulers will be needed to judge and settle arguments. Remember, Satan will be released at the end of this thousand-year period. He will gather those who during the Millennium reject God for who He is and follow Satan to a certain end by living in the Lake of Burning Sulfur. Our God is a God of multiple chances.

The last words we read as we stop to get a quick glance of what heaven will be like and those who will be there, the sentence in verse 17 says, *"and God will wipe away every tear from their eyes."* What a wonderful thought to carry on through our life while here on earth.

CHAPTER 12

Satan Battles the Archangel Michael

Read – Chapter 12:1-4

This story begins in heaven and will end up on the earth very quickly. The woman we read about represents the mother of Jesus. The twelve stars represent the Tribes of Israel. We are reading an analogy of the Jewish nation that is about to be restored back into the good graces of God their Father. The nation of Israel was about to give birth to the Son of God. A Son, by the way, they would reject even through today. This also gives us a picture of what has happened to the nation of Israel. Israel's Messiah was rejected for the most part by a major percentage of Jews around Jerusalem. Since that time, Jews have been scattered all over the world, but soon will return to a place of safety. They are given warnings to go out of the cities and hide in places God will show them.

In verse three we read about another sign in heaven that represents Satan. Later in this chapter we will read about a heavenly battle against Satan. Now, Satan is angry in heaven and the Bible says that his tail swept one-third of the stars from heaven. Of course, Satan did not literally throw one-third of the stars to earth. If that were to happen, we would be dead and this world would have exploded, stopping the Wrath of God from taking place. The one-third of the stars represents one-third of the Believers on earth abandoning their place in heaven by following the antichrist, Satan's christ. The church has been warned to be ready for all these things to happen. However, many antichrist's, although appearing to be right on every Biblical issue, defraud the people and cause them to think they will not have to suffer any of the persecution that awaits a church of Christ in a rebellious world. Are you beginning to see where these messages of caution for Believers contain words that are hard on our ears? No one wants to hear that they will suffer for Christ, or any one else. The church MUST understand that they have to take responsibility for their salvation and heed the warnings of Jesus. (1 Peter 2:21 / Philippians 1:29-30)

Satan wanted to capture and kill the baby that the woman would deliver. Satan lost that battle with Jesus described to us in Matthew long ago, and he will lose his battle with an archangel in heaven now. The bad news for Israel is they will suffer as Satan is hurled to the earth.

Please pay close attention to the description of Satan here in these verses; one character described as a woman represents the nation of Israel. Satan is described here as a huge red dragon with seven heads and ten horns. Notice that there are three more crowns than heads. The extra three crowns were of defeated nations that would be turned over to the antichrist very soon. We will read more about the ten horns later in the book of Daniel. I understand that this can seem very convoluted. What we are reading comes from one event already completed and the other that would take place shortly. You will get a clearer picture as we complete THE END. The nation of Israel would be protected as well for 1,260 days (42 months).

What we are reading will eventually lead us to a struggle for the power of the Throne Room in Heaven and the power of God Himself. Now the physical fight begins in heaven. God has always given Satan access to the Throne Room as we have read many times. God's Throne has been Satan's deep desire from the moment he separated himself from God when he was a heavenly angel. It must have looked easy for Satan as he watched God create the world and all who are in it. If God can do this from heaven, what would stop him from having that same power? Of course, all he would have to do was to defeat God and take over the Throne. Satan finds out that it would only take a mighty angel like Michael and his angels to throw him and his followers out of heaven.

At this point God has denied Satan's access to heaven through the archangel Michael and his angels. Now the earth will have Satan bound by God to be on the earth only and not roaming the heavens (Job

1:6-7). His anger will be intensified as he deals with the population left for him on earth, which will include God's chosen people (the Jewish nation). We are not given the time of this battle, but we can compare timed events that will tell us when this happens. (Refer to notes at the end of this chapter). Now, I know we could haggle about exactly when this war happens, but really now, can anyone say with confidence when the heavenly battle will take place and Satan will be thrown to earth for good? In the following verse we read about the importance of standing firm in the faith of their God, no matter what the cost, no matter when Jesus comes.

1 Peter 5:8-9...*Be self-controlled and alert. Your enemy <u>the devil prowls around</u> like a roaring lion <u>looking for someone to devour</u>. Resist him, standing firm in the faith, because you know that your brothers <u>throughout the world</u> are undergoing the <u>same kind of sufferings</u>.*

Read – Chapter 12:5-6

As we read about the story of Satan trying to kill Jesus immediately after His birth, we remember that Satan tried to kill Jesus again by offering Him the world after Christ became obedient to baptism (Luke Chapter 4:1-11). Satan knew that he had to make a move on God trying to dislodge God from the Throne. In fact, we will read shortly, Satan could not even defeat the Archangel Michael and his angels in a battle against Satan and his angels. In this text, we read about the efforts of Satan who made at least three attempts before and during the life of Christ to kill Him. We are reminded again of what Satan would do to try to take over the power of the Throne Room of God, and that Satan chose this moment in time to overthrow God as the Creator of this world.

As we read this, John is describing events sometime during the Tribulation period. Satan would no longer have admittance to heaven and the Godhead. Please let me explain one more time about the story of one- third of the stars being swept to earth by Satan. This represents the number of Believers who will give up their secure position in heaven. Although Jesus had warned them repeatedly of the power of the antichrist, many in the church thought they had been exempted from the Tribulation because of the false prophets who, although preaching Christ crucified, fell into the trap of Satan by assuring their congregations that they would be caught-up before all hell breaks lose on earth. What a tragic situation this will be as we see those who thought they had a place in heaven learn that they have been deceived by their religious leaders. We know this to be the intent of this language because if one-third of the stars were to hit the earth, the explosion would obliterate the earth before further judgments and wrath was scheduled to ravage the population. After being thrown out of heaven, Satan will be on a terror and will use all the evil at his disposal to draw people toward his evil thinking.

What these verses give us is a brief description of what Satan is doing and what he has done to defeat God in heaven. From the birth of Christ, to the closing of the door of access to heaven and God, this story enrages the Dragon.

Notice in this verse that the child (Jesus) was snatched up to God in His Throne Room, which is where He is at this very moment. We look back for a moment at the confirmation of the birth and resurrection of Christ. The description of the events with the mother of this child represents the protection that will be given to the Jewish Nation as they take cover from the antichrist that deceived them through a broken peace treaty with those countries around them. Once the antichrist has revealed who he really is, it will be too late for the Christian community to take back the Mark of the Beast and return to the safety in the arms of Jesus. Israel will have fled the attack of Satan who will do all he can to destroy those whom Christ loves. The hand of God will shelter this nation for 42 months. As Satan finally realizes the effort to destroy God's people has eluded him and his time is short, he will turn his attention over to those belonging to God. Remember that once Michael and his angels throw Satan out of heaven, the Devil will be extremely angry and search out every person he can to entice them over to the side of evil. Upon leaving the safety of their God, these people will be exposed to the antichrist that has won many Believers over to Satan's side. Many in the church who have not already taken the "Mark of the Beast" will be forced to take the mark immediately after the antichrist has been revealed. These Believers will follow the antichrist to their eternal death in the Burning Lake of Sulfur.

Read – Chapter 12:7

It was always the intent of Satan to steal the Throne in Heaven from God as we read in Isaiah 14:12-15. He thought he was stronger than God was and that his position as the most beautiful angel would cause a majority of other angels to follow him. He convinced many of the angels in heaven to follow him. Some became demons while others ended up in the Abyss to wait for judgment and punishment leading to eternal life in the Lake of Burning Sulfur. As it turns out, Satan could not even defeat Michael and his angels for a position in heaven.

Isaiah 14:12-15...*How you have fallen from heaven, O morning star, son of the dawn! You have been cast down to the earth, you who once laid low the nations! You said in your heart, "I will ascend to heaven; I will raise my throne above the stars of God; I will sit enthroned on the mount of assembly, on the utmost heights of the sacred mountain. I will ascend above the tops of the clouds; I will make myself like the Most High." But you are brought down to the grave, to the depths of the pit.*

It is clear from the earlier passage that Satan has had access to the Throne of God up until this time. We can affirm this by reading the story of Job. Since Satan lost the battle in heaven for the position of God, you know that he will fight vigorously to defeat the Son and all those who follow Him. Satan will also fight to steal the place in heaven you were predestined to fill by your decision to follow Jesus and to spend eternity with Him. He has won millions of battles with the human beings of this earth. He has stolen many Believers by infiltrating the church with many antichrists.

This battle takes place in heaven. If Satan could win the battle in heaven, there would be no war here on earth. Satan loses the battle, but will live another day to fight for the Throne of God on earth.

Read – Chapter 12:9

Satan loses his access to heaven. He knows he is confined to earth to deceive many by leading people away from God. Satan has already deceived many. Many of the readers of this study will reject Jesus as their Savior. How important it is to look at Jesus for the second time. Satan will spend many hours up until this time to accuse the saints or Believers of being weak followers. Of course, many accusations have been made from Satan to God about His family. I believe that some of us may be guilty of holding others more accountable for their lives when confessing Christ as their Savior. During these times it will be critical for the church to come together and overcome an angry Satan who will do will he can to steal our life with Christ Jesus. It would be wise for us to remember that Satan could not even defeat the angel Michael. How in the world could he defeat God, and that same God is the One we worship today. The persecution of the coming tribulation days will be overwhelming and we will have to count on the power of the Holy Spirit living within each one of us. Jesus talks to us about the importance of unity within His family; let's work on that aspect of our relationship with each other.

I would like to say this one more time because it is so important. If you think you have been attacked by evil because of your disobedience to God and guilt overtakes you at times, wait until Satan loses his position of access to God. Those days will take on more intense pressure to draw those who are left of mankind to him. All these years Satan believed he would finally take over the Throne of God and reign himself forever. Satan will feel like he is in an earthly prison and now he is extremely angry.

Read – Chapter 12:10-11

No more will Satan or his demons have access to the Throne Room of God to question your salvation and to challenge God for your soul. Three things made it possible for the followers of Christ to be overcomers. The first is they accepted that the blood of Jesus was able to cleanse them from all sin. The second is that they were not afraid to testify of what Christ had done for them, and thirdly they did not love their own life over the love for their Savior.

There is no doubt that we are approaching the end of the Tribulation period as we read this text. Both Jew and Gentile alike will have overcome the temptations and persecutions from the devil and his angels. We have to love God so much that our love for ourselves becomes secondary to that of God. We must be able to stand firm to the end.

It is hard understand why people are having such a hard time accepting Christ. Can't they see that governments, cities, and people are fighting the Throne Room of God? If they are fighting it so desperately, there must be something to it. They would prefer that God just go away and leave them to their own devices.

Read – Chapter 12:12

The persecution intensifies as we get closer and closer to the end. Now we have an angry devil and he will turn up the pressure attacking those who know Christ as their Savior if we are still here on earth. The time is very short. Satan will attack with a vengeance and never stop trying to destroy Christian lives until he sees Christ coming to earth. Remember though, Believers have been marked by God and the time of persecution will be cut short resulting in us going to live with Christ forever.

Read – Chapter 12:13-14

Now the time has come for the nation of Israel to accept Christ Jesus as their Messiah. Some may see the two wings of an eagle as an aircraft that will take the woman and her son to the wilderness to hide out. Actually, the woman and the son will appear to Satan as a vision of what began the process of the freedom of the nation of Israel to finally accept their Messiah. The pressure will be so intense now on God's chosen people that they would not survive were it not for their God. The nation of Israel has always taken the rough road to God. They, like us, fight the highs and the lows of living a purely godly life.

Read – Chapter 12:15-16

Here Satan causes a huge flood to occur in hopes of killing the Nation of Israel, but God causes an earthquake to swallow up the water. This flood is the evil coming from Satan to engulf the world and make him an all-powerful god. However, God's power is demonstrated once again to the people He loves that He is in control. No matter what Satan can throw at you, you can overcome. Remember, as a Born-Again Believer you are a child of God, and God does not lose even one of His family, unless of course, we choose to abandon Him. It sometimes takes great courage to stand up for Jesus, but the rewards are magnificent and your joy will be complete for time and eternity if you just stand firm in your faith.

Read – Chapter 12:17

After God protects the nation of Israel and the Son of God, Satan turns his attention to those believers who are left around the world. May God give His strength to those who will have to go through the torment and persecution of the evil of Satan.

Believers will have to stand up for Jesus and overcome the temptations and persecution that will come. Another war will take place on earth between the evils of the satanic godhead and the Believers that are here during the Tribulation. I know I have said this many times before, but I want to say it again; there is no excuse for a Believer failing the test of their soul. Our strength comes from Christ who has promised that He will stand between evil and us. There is a warning for us in verse 12b of this chapter. The warning is that Satan, after being defeated, will come at the Believers with more energy than before (*"Satan is filled with fury, because he knows his time is short"*).

Jesus said to us, *"But woe to the earth and the sea because the devil has gone down to you."* The devil will soon be inviting the antichrist and the False Prophet to join him in battle. The goal will be to discourage and trick Believers into following these evil friends of the Beast. The master impersonator of goodness, mercy and sympathy will draw people to himself by performing the same miracles as the Christ. Even the church will be deceived and many think that is impossible. If they cannot talk you out of your salvation, they will try to pry it out of your soul. It is so important that all of us be prepared every minute of our remaining lives for the evil that seeks to rob us of our souls. I understand that this may sound melodramatic, but the assault on the Church will be something that we could never imagine, unless we stay in the Scriptures.

WHEN WILL THESE EVENTS HAPPEN?

NOTES: When attempting to put the events of Revelation into the proper alignment, we must use the reference in the Book of Daniel as he describes the length of the Tribulation, Daniel 9:27. *"One Seven"* represents seven years. Many events are described using the mid-point of the Tribulation as *"time, times, and half a time."* This is broken down to 42 months or 1260 days. (See Below).

Daniel 7:25

He will speak against the Most High and oppress his holy people and try to change the set times and the laws. The holy people will be delivered into his hands for a time, times and half a time.

The events in Chapter Twelve most likely happen at or near the Mid-Tribulation point. Several hints in this chapter lead us to believe that the antichrist has ruled for one-half of the Tribulation. Because of the efforts of the antichrist to successfully bring together the nations around Israel to sign a peace treaty, and other miracles performed by this man, it is possible that millions of Believers have been deceived by the antichrist into accepting the "Mark of the Beast." Know this, the time for repentance is extremely short at this time. Adding to the pressure of the False Prophet making all people accept the "Mark." Satan will use his power to increase that demand.

CHAPTER 13

The Beast and the False Prophet

Read – Chapter 13:1-3

In this chapter, we will be reading about the Beast and the False Prophet. The Beast is the antichrist that will play a major role during the Tribulation as Satan gives him authority to accomplish evil in his name. The False Prophet is the hooligan in evil's counterfeit godhead. He will be the one who forces people to take the "Mark of the Beast" near the Mid-Tribulation point. Here we see the Dragon (Satan) standing aside as the Beast (antichrist) comes from the earth's population to assume the role that he was meant to play for the Dragon. The description of the antichrist challenges our ability to think in the abstract for an explanation of his appearance. The ten horns that are accredited to the antichrist are symbolic of ten nations that are under his control. We will read later in our study that several of the horns are damaged because he has quickly taken them over.

When reading of ten horns, seven heads, and ten crowns it is easy to get confused. The only way to have peace about all these things, speaking of horns, heads, and crowns, is to do a separate study that includes the book of Daniel and other prophets in the Old Testament. Finding out the meaning of some of these things comes down to supposition rather than fact. If you are concerned about horns, crowns, heads, and other unusual descriptions of End Time things and you feel uncomfortable about the conclusions I have made, I understand. I pray that you will continue your study of the Revelation of Christ until you come to peace with the conclusions you have made. Do not rely on my conclusions or the conclusions of others. Keep in prayer with the Holy Spirit who will show you the answers and will give you the peace you are looking for. Please allow me to remind you to not worry too much about the number of heads, eyes, etc.

Related Verse(s) / Daniel 7:24...*The ten horns are ten kings who will come from this kingdom. After them another king will arise, different from the earlier ones; he will subdue three kings. He will speak against the Most High and oppress his saints and try to change the set times and the laws. The saints will be handed over to him for a time, times and half a time.*

I hope you have taken note of the description of the heads of this beast. As the Scripture tells of the blasphemous names written on the heads, I pray that you will realize the absolute wickedness of this minister of Satan. Blaspheming the name of God was aimed falsely at Christ and to Steven, plus other Disciples of Christ as they taught the Gospel. Of course, all those charges were a lie.

It is important to understand that the antichrist will quietly increase persecution on the saints for 42 months. At the end of this 42-month period, he will turn into the most evil tyrant you can imagine. We will talk more about the timing of the Great Tribulation as we investigate this 7-year period. The reference to the "sea" in this text symbolizes an evil being called the antichrist coming to infiltrate and control the minds of those committed to Christ. He will be a force to be reckoned with during the seven years of the Tribulation. The following notes are based on my conclusions.

Notes...

1. The seven heads are seven kings or leaders of a ten part Empire of Rome. Three of the kings would immediately turn their kingdoms over to the antichrist.
2. Satan has given the ten kings a crown of power to rule the earth, but all authority has been given to the Beast.
3. The penalty for blasphemy against God, Christ, and the Holy Spirit is death. Satan knows that, and defies the power of God by using blasphemy on everything he does during the Tribulation;

even though he has just been defeated by Michael and his angels for a place in heaven. We begin to see Satan as a desperate evil force as he increases his malice.

Acts 6:11…*Then they secretly persuaded some men to say, "We have heard Stephen speak <u>words of blasphemy</u> against Moses and <u>against God</u>."*

<u>Who is the Antichrist?</u>

Any antichrist is to be noted and identified to the church family. Of course the antichrist we want to study now is The Antichrist that will kill many Christians, and try to overthrow God. The antichrist is the christ of Satan. Satan has set up his kingdom here on earth that mirrors the Throne Room of God. 1 John 4:3 tells us that he is here on this earth right this very minute. Satan sees himself to be God, the antichrist is the replacement for Christ Jesus, and the False Prophet plays the role of the Holy Spirit. This war from the counterfeit godhead toward the Godhead of the Father, Son, and Holy Spirit at this point will soon be over. The main concern of the church is how many of their numbers will be duped into believing the antichrist and end up taking the Mark of the Beast. We do know that at least one third of the church will fall into the trap Satan has set for Believers. They followed their religious leaders without reading the Scriptures for themselves and learning the truth about the gathering of the saints.

Related Verse(s) / <u>Revelation 13:5-6</u>…*The beast was given a mouth to utter proud words and blasphemies and to exercise his authority for forty-two months. He opened his mouth to blaspheme God, and to slander his name and his dwelling place and those who live in heaven.*

The antichrist that we are concerned with sets up an image of himself in the Temple, and the False Prophet will make sure all people worship that image. Those who refuse to take the Mark of the Beast will be beheaded. The antichrist is given power from Satan to act on his behalf. Normally that thought would terrify us. However, the power that was given to the antichrist was impotent to use against any of the saints unless God allowed it to happen. There is a group of people who will be immune to the power of the antichrist and they are the Believers whose names have been written in the Book of Life. Of course, they will be exposed to some of the atrocities of the end times, but the time for those things will be cut short for those special Believers who have not given in to evil, and stood up for Christ no matter what the consequences.

As we look at many of the churches today, we see them in turmoil from time to time. Some of the people who cause trouble in the church will leave, and others will stay and cause trouble in the church for years. Many of us have already seen what the local antichrists can do to a community church.

Let me repeat that John seems to identify and call those who leave the church as antichrists. If we read further in this same chapter, we will see that even those who deny that Jesus is the Christ of God are called antichrists. Once again, the antichrist that we are referring to sets up an image of himself in the Temple as the False Prophet enforces a new law saying all people must worship that image or suffer persecution beyond their imagination. Others who refuse to take the Mark of the Beast will be lose their heads if they do not bow down to the idol of the antichrist. To believe that the Lord's church will not have to suffer for Him are in terrible trouble.

Related Verse(s) / <u>Revelation 20:4</u>…*I saw thrones on which were seated those who had been given authority to judge. And I saw the souls of those who had been **beheaded** because of their testimony for Jesus and because of the word of God. They had not worshiped the beast or his image and had not received his mark on their foreheads or their hands. They came to life and reigned with Christ a thousand years.*

The focus of the first three and a half years of the Tribulation will begin with the preparation of the worst disaster that this world and its people will ever experience. At first, the antichrist will bring this world out of chaos and establish peace and prosperity. However, Jesus will be ready to unleash his punishment against the people who have turned their backs on Him. I do not know when Jesus will begin his Judgment of this world, but I do know how it will start. You can know that time as well. There are many theories about this timing, which is why it is so important that we stay in the Scriptures and pay attention to what is happening in our world.

Much of the second three and a half years will be a battle of God versus evil. The world has now lost their opportunity to accept Christ as the church has been harvested to heaven. Looking back in time, to the beginning of the Tribulation, the church will be under severe persecution. Our responsibility during this time will be to gain strength by reading the Word of God and stay faithful to Christ keeping in constant prayer for His guidance. It will also be important that the church bands together for support and comfort.

Read – Chapter 13:4

Again, we see the antichrist with a similar look of our Savior. He will have power to do miracles. This man who seems to be Jesus will deceive many in the churches. We have all seen men and women who practiced deception and magic as if it was really happening. However, this man will be filled with evil, but appear to be a saint. At the point of Mid-Tribulation, the antichrist will have a depraved mouth, which he will use to blaspheme Jesus. He will astound Christians with his power.

Related Verse(s) / Matthew 24:4-5…*Jesus answered: "Watch out that no one deceives you. For many will come in my name, claiming, 'I am the Christ,' and will deceive many.*

Notice that the people followed the antichrist because Satan had given the antichrist authority. That proclamation promotes the antichrist to a position that will result in most of society following him. Then when the antichrist calls down fire from heaven and performs other so-called miracles, even many in the church will elect to follow him and give up their position in the eternal family of God to follow a counterfeit. Jesus had warned them to be careful and not go out after everyone identifying themselves as the Christ. Once again, we see the lesson of what can happen if the church stops reading the Bible and depends on their pastor to do it for them. The consequences will be devastating. (2 Timothy 4:2-3)

Related Verse(s) / Matthew 24:23-25…*At that time if anyone says to you, 'Look, here is the Christ!' or, 'There he is!' do not believe it. For false christs and false prophets will appear and perform great signs and miracles to deceive even the elect--if that were possible. See, I have told you ahead of time.*

Points to Consider

1. Notice that the beast was <u>given authority</u> for about seven years. Nothing happens in this world or the world to come without the authority of God.
2. The only thing coming out of the mouth of this evil thing was words blaspheming the Savior.

The power of the antichrist is only authorized for about seven years. The last three and a half years will eventually see the total destruction of the entire world. When we read about the "Seal Judgments," the "Trumpet Judgments," and the "Wrath of God," we will come to understand that peace once again has been taken from the world. The peace treaty that the antichrist set up for the first forty-two months of the Tribulation period with Israel will be broken. The False Prophet will demand that all people take the "Mark of the Beast." Once that mark has been put on the body, it cannot be removed. Jesus has said that no one who accepts the mark will enter the kingdom of God (Revelation 14:9-10).

Read – Chapter 13:5-6

I pray you will understand the gravity of the situation. Here comes a man on the scene that turns chaos into peace, confusion into calm and impending war into world peace. I cannot think of a time in history that this evil man would not be accepted as a peacemaker and some would even call him a god. Over times past, we have seen men in positions of authority who gave the appearance of being fair and having good character, only to see them show their evil side after time passes by.

The problem here is that he turns on the nation of Israel and the saints living on earth during this time after the first three and a half years. The antichrist is given power to overcome the saints as we enter the Mid- Tribulation period. Everyone will worship him except those who belong to Christ Jesus. This is going to be a tremendous challenge to those Christians going through this time. This is why what Christ said to the churches is so important. The overwhelming theme in His messages was to overcome, to hang on until the end. Let's pray that the church begins to prepare for these terrible times. The Revelation of Christ Jesus was meant for us to read and follow.

Related Verse(s) / <u>Revelation 22:16</u>...*I, Jesus, have sent my angel to* <u>*give you this testimony **for the churches***</u>*. I am the Root and the Offspring of David, and the bright Morning Star."*

Again, let me remind you that the Dragon or Satan will give his power over to the antichrist. To validate his power, the antichrist will call fire down from heaven. He will also do many miracles imitating Christ Jesus. The antichrist will shout out vicious names to God and the Son of God. Included in this behavior will be slander of heavenly creatures and angels.

Read – Chapter 13:7-10

Note in the verse above that Jesus says He has sent this testimony for all the churches. What some people are suggesting is that we can take a pair of scissors and cut out Chapter 5 through Chapter 21. How ignorant is such a statement? Anyone believing this statement is an antichrist. If you know such a person, run as fast as you can away from this heresy.

Points to Consider

1. The antichrist is given power to make war against us.
2. Absolutely no one will escape war without Christ.
3. If our name is written in the Lamb's Book of Life, victory is ours with Christ.
   a) They can put us in prison
   b) They can kill us with the sword
   c) But we will overcome!

4. If we do not hold on to Christ then we can be counted with those who will turn their backs on Him.

Related Verse(s) / <u>Matthew 24:10-13</u>...At that time, many will turn away from the faith and will betray and hate each other, and many false prophets will appear and deceive many people. Because increase of wickedness, the love of most will grow cold, but he who stands firm to the end will be saved.

Can you see this developing in our world today? Our world has been saturated with evil people who desire to stamp out the name of Christ Jesus and ALL those who claim to be His. When Jesus does not come for His church as many modern Christian leaders have proclaimed, they will be responsible for millions of Christians doubting their salvation and following what seems to be the Christ. Only he will be the antichrist and destroy those millions of Christians.

The hate level we have seen over the last two election cycles in this country have been filled with venomous tongues of hateful people. The hate level will increase and even those who once knew us in a church setting will turn on us and betray us to officials who will be watching for locations where the followers of Christ are meeting. Ladies and gentlemen, this is a serious situation. Please remember, you are responsible for your relationship with Christ, not your pastor or spiritual leader. If someone is telling you that you will not have to go through the Tribulation period, ask him or her to prove it, and then read for yourself what the Scriptures say.

Read – Chapter 13:11-12

Notice that the beast appears to be as gentle as a lamb and that he mirrors the Christ of God. The word out of his mouth gives him away as a tyrant and the voice of evil. Where does this great power of the antichrist come from? The power of the false prophet is given to him by the antichrist. This should explain the evil that has infiltrated the world to touch every single human being.

Points to Consider

1. This beast is the one called "The antichrist"
2. He becomes the strong-arm manager of the Dragon
3. He will act like the Lamb of God for a time, but he will be a counterfeit christ with evil on his mind

Read Chapter 13:13

I must admit it will be very difficult to resist the antichrist when he first appears. He will be so charismatic that it will be a challenge to reject him. Plus the systems he will be initiating will make sense for our society and promise a worldwide peace and financial security. The False Prophet will be given the same power as the antichrist. Between the both of them, it will be easy to defraud the Christian community, especially after being lied to about the rapture of the church prior to the Tribulation.

Related Verse(s) / Revelation 19:20…But the beast was captured, and with him the false prophet who had performed the miraculous signs on his behalf. With these signs he had deluded those who had received the mark of the beast and worshiped his image. The two of them were thrown alive into the fiery lake of burning sulfur.

Read – Chapter 13:14-15

Here is the proof of just how much power the False Prophet has. Although this False Prophet is supposed to represent the attributes of the Holy Spirit, he fails in truth. His approach is strong handed and has the threat of death with it. He does not convict by the conscience to follow the antichrist, but instead uses force and threats to make people worship the image of the antichrist.

1. The False Prophet will do the same thing.
2. The False Prophet will deceive many of the saints.
3. Here is the dynamic duo in action that will wreak havoc worldwide.

Now there has been an image set up in a wing of the Temple to have the world bow down and worship this image. What will the Christian community do? The Bible says that many will fall away from their salvation and follow the counterfeit godhead. That road will lead to a place called the Lake of Burning Sulfur, and people will live in that lake for eternity. They will not see rest, but only torment. There will never be a time when they can rethink their position and accept Jesus. There is only one time to do that, and that is right now!

Read – Chapter 13:16-17

Now we do not read about this False Prophet until later in the book of Revelation, and it is in the middle of the Tribulation. The mark referred to in this text is an order given by the False Prophet to ALL people to take the mark. However, this mark has been given on a voluntary basis for three and a half years earlier as the Tribulation begins. Now that we have crossed over the line of the Mid-Tribulation period, we will take the "Mark" or struggle to live day by day.

Points to Consider

1. At that time, believers will have to choose life or death.
2. Eternal life with Christ Life by not taking the Mark.
3. Taking the mark will mean eternal torment.
4. Taking the mark will mean that the person will experience the second death.
5. Refusing the mark will mean a person will not experience a second death, and live with God forever.

Read – Chapter 13:18 Points to Consider

1. We know that evil has a trinity. It is made up of Satan, the Antichrist, and the False Prophet.
2. Who is identified with the number 666?

Many names have been suggested as the one representing the antichrist. I do not know yet or understand the meaning of the number 666 as it relates to the person of evil. I have read several theories concerning how to identify the antichrist; but to be honest; all of them lack the biblical wherewithal. I give my theory of the number of man as 666 below. I know that the number three is an imperfect number, and the human nature of man is given that number. If we add up the counterfeit godhead, we come up with the number 666. The number three certainly can apply to all three of the false godhead and certainly will add up to the number of man.

Satan's number 3	Antichrist number................3
Man's number .... <u>3</u>	Man's number......................<u>3</u>
= 6	= 6

False Prophet's..................3
Man's number..................<u>3</u>
               = 6

Total = <u>666</u>

CHAPTER 14

Looking Back / The Harvesting of the Saints

Read – Chapter 14:1-2

Standing before the Throne of God stood 144,000 Jews that would be at the Messiah's side for eternity. They were a remnant chosen by the <u>Father</u> to be with their Messiah. This very special relationship is an example of what the nation of Israel as a whole could have had if they only would have obeyed and honored the commands of God. We read earlier about the 144,000 Jews who were marked to <u>serve with the</u> <u>Lord</u>. They were a representation of the twelve tribes of Israel. These men; 12,000 from each tribe, were special in that they were virgins and their hearts were pure.

Related Verse(s) / <u>Revelation 7:3</u>…*"Do not harm the land or the sea or the trees until <u>we put a seal</u> on the foreheads of the servants of our God."*

An obvious celebration was taking place in heaven. Who can know the number of harps being played, but we can imagine the sound of the power of rushing waters. We have seen what that power can do. Close your eyes and listen to the beautiful harps playing their harmony as the Godhead listens to the music. This event gives us a little peek of what heaven will be like. Heaven will be a blissful place in which peace and harmony will be the order of eternity.

Read – Chapter 14:3-5

Why could only the 144,000 learn this song? It was because they were pure in God's eyes. Because they were so close to Christ in their worship and adoration of Him, they refused to defile themselves with anyone, including taking on wives. They were virgins. "Pure and blameless" are the words of our Lord when describing them. Only they could sing this new song.

Who could offer themselves to God as having never lied and devoted themselves to the Lord? Christ has always put spiritually pure men in positions of authority even as some of those men were able to come out of the personal traumas of life while engrossed in sin. For these 144,000 men, it was standing in a pure position for the Godhead throughout eternity. For those who will lose their life for Christ during the Tribulation period, it will mean a 1,000 year reign with Christ Jesus during the Millennium. For us who love the Lord and do what He has asked of us, Jesus gives us Paradise until the New Jerusalem will be resting on a New Earth.

Let's take a look at just a couple of men who made terrible mistakes in their lives. One was called a favorite of Jesus; the other was a killer who was called to be an Apostle to the Gentiles.

Related Verse(s) / 2 Samuel 7:9…God's promise to **David**; *I have been with you wherever you have gone, and I have cut off all your enemies from before you. Now I will make your name great, like the names of the greatest men of the earth.* See Chapters 10; 11; 12…

Acts 9:3-4 / Jesus chooses **Paul** to be a great Apostle even after trying to shut down the church of Christ Jesus…*As he neared Damascus on his journey, suddenly a light from heaven flashed around him. He fell to the ground and heard a voice say to him, "Saul, Saul, why do you persecute me?"*

All of us owe Paul for the courage he demonstrated as he approached the other Apostles who had been with Jesus during His ministry. Paul's obedience to the Lord gave us an opportunity to be in the family of God.

BACK TO OUR TEXT

Read – Chapter 14:6-7

The First Angel

How do you suppose we will be able to identify this angel flying in midair, and how will everyone see him? In our world today, we are able to see events as they happen through television feeds from the four corners of this earth. We watch a spaceship go off the launch pad in Florida and continue to watch that vehicle until it is outside of our atmosphere. It would not be a stretch to say that every news station in the world would carry an angel flying around the sky giving us a warning to fear God. This event is described to us in the book of Matthew.

Related Verse(s) / Matthew 24:14…*And this gospel of the kingdom will be preached in the whole world as a testimony to all nations, and then the end will come.*

The important thing is not the angel flying around, but the message he is carrying. His message is a grave one. He is giving the world one last chance to accept Jesus the Christ. If not, they will pay a terrible price for their disobedience. At this point, the world is nearing the end of its existence. The Harvesting of the Saints is about to take place. God is giving the creation one last warning to believe in His Son Jesus and to accept Him as their Savior. We should be telling everyone we can about the saving Grace of the Lord.

Read – Chapter 14:8

The Second Angel

Babylon, of course, was the conqueror over Israel and took the people of God into captivity long ago in 586 B.C. And Babylon would pay a terrible price for that action. They not only conquered the nation of Israel, but they turned the nation of Israel into what Babylon represented. Babylon had among their customs to sacrifice their children to one of their gods. It was a nation of sexual immorality. This was also a very rich area, not only in gold and silver, but also in fertile land. Instead of using these wonderful resources to serve the Lord, King Nebuchadnezzar used it to conqueror Jerusalem and to bring about such an evil society that God would make mention of this horrible city, and the evil it spread throughout the world. Babylon even took the articles in the Temple of God and used them in ungodly ways. There was no way that God would not punish this city with all the Wrath of Heaven.

Related Verse(s) / 2 Kings 24:10...*At that time the officers of Nebuchadnezzar king of Babylon advanced on Jerusalem and laid siege to it, and Nebuchadnezzar himself came up to the city while his officers were besieging it.*

2 **Kings 24:13**...*As the LORD had declared, Nebuchadnezzar removed all the treasures from the temple of the LORD and from the royal palace, and took away all the gold articles that Solomon king of Israel had made for the temple of the LORD.*

Read – Chapter 14:9-11

The Third Angel

While the antichrist is convincing people to take on the Mark of the Beast, this angel is proclaiming that taking the Mark will end in the Wrath of God directed squarely on them. The Lake of Burning Sulfur awaits all those who reject Jesus and take the Mark. Christ, along with His angels, will look upon those who rejected Him as they thrash about in torment forever. There is a price to pay for bad decisions and behavior. There is no doubt that many people believe that rejecting Christ is not a bad thing to do. Many believe that there is no God, but if there was a God He would not hurt His creation. Once people have received the Mark of the Beast, they have assured themselves an eternity of torment and an eternity without rest. It is essential that we get the message out, that Christ Jesus is Lord and He wants to have a relationship with all people. If they refuse to listen, then we must move on to others who may listen and accept Christ.

Related Verse(s) / Matthew 10:14-15…*If anyone will not welcome you or listen to your words, shake the dust off your feet when you leave that home or town. I tell you the truth; it will be more bearable for Sodom and Gomorrah on the Day of Judgment than for that town.*

Read – Chapter 14:12-13

We are obviously near the end of the Judgments brought upon this earth by Christ. It will not be long after this third angel speaks when Jesus will send His angels to harvest His family. Your eternal life with the Lord hangs on this one verse if you are still here on earth during this period. We must have a patient endurance to hang on until the end just before God gives orders for the Vial or Bowl Wraths. People will be warned one final time that they cannot take the Mark of the Beast, nor will anyone get away with denying the name of Christ Jesus. The essentials of life will be taken away from us who refuse to take the Mark. We cannot take the mark even for the sake of food or health, and we cannot worship any other god than the One who is in heaven. Death will be a blessing for those Believers who are left during the end of the judgments. Others will seek death, but nothing they do to themselves will end in death.

Related Verse(s) / Revelation 9:6 - *During those days men will seek death, but will not find it; they will long to die, but death will elude them.* How long, if ever, will it take the majority of people realize that we are in trouble and the end is drawing near?

Read – Chapter 14:14-16

Harvesting of the Saints Detailed

At the end of this chapter, we see the proof that eternal life is for everyone. The question is this: when it becomes Harvest time, will you be gathered up with Christ or Satan? Will you be in the loving arms of Christ Jesus?

Related Verse(s) / Matthew 13:38-39…*The weeds are the sons of the evil one and the enemy who sows them is the devil. The harvest is the end of the age, and the harvesters are angels.*

Here we see that everyone has had the opportunity to be "Born-Again" through the blood of Christ that was shed on the cross for all. You will notice that the angel issuing the order to reap says that the harvest is ripe. Accepting the Lord for who He is was an easy thing to do prior to this Harvest but most refused the offer of the Lord. Now people will endure torment beyond imagination through the Wrath of God. It will be too late. The people left after the Harvest will no doubt have hardened hearts. I am sure that after a few days in the Lake of Burning Sulfur, people will be seeking a way out of the torment. There will NEVER be that opportunity again.

Remember, we are looking back to the event given to us in Chapter 11. In the example of the Gathering of the Saints and the destruction of the grapes (sinners), both of these events happen in concert with each other. The Harvesting of the Saints takes place, and immediately after that, the people left on earth will suffer the consequences of the Wrath of God. People have had many warnings yet they ignored the warnings of the Bowl/Vial Wrath, which will result in horrible torment without end. Now, if you want to hold on to the thought about being raptured into heaven, this would be the place for doing just that. As the Wrath of God is about to happen, our Lord through His angels, will harvest those Believers who are still on this earth. If you are on this earth during this time, I am positive that you will find yourself thankful for the decision you made to accept the grace and love of God through His Son.

It should be pointed out here that the verses below could not be used to support a Pre-Tribulation Rapture theory. If we keep everything in context, we can see that God is talking about the decision-making process that results in a decision to accept or reject Him. He sent angels to warn us of impending doom in the previous chapter. He then tells us what will be the result of the decision we make to accept Him and His ways. There is a penalty for rejecting Him.

Related Verse(s) / 2 Peter 3:10-12…*But the day of the Lord will come like a thief. The heavens will disappear with a roar; the elements will be destroyed by fire, and the earth and everything in it will be laid bare. Since everything will be destroyed in this way, what kind of people ought you to be? You ought to live holy and godly lives as you look forward to the day of God and speed its coming. That day will bring about the destruction of the heavens by fire, and the elements will melt in the heat.*

__1 Peter 5:10__... And the God of all grace, who called you to his eternal glory in Christ, <u>after you have suffered a little while</u>, will himself <u>restore you and make you strong, firm and steadfast.</u>

<u>Read – Chapter 14:17-20</u>

Finally, those who did not heed the warning are brought together and are subject to the full Wrath of God. Can you imagine someone turning down the love of God, a God who created them and the earth, for an eternity in darkness, torment, and no rest? Have you ever been in a position where you have had to stay up for hours and hours without rest? Do you remember the way you felt? You could have slept standing up, but in hell, you will never rest. This is serious business! Please make sure your family members and friends know what will happen if they continue to neglect Christ. Another important thing to remember is that Born-Again Believers will go through two-thirds of the Tribulation period. We will be saved from the "Wrath of God," but will experience the effects of the Judgments of Christ. I understand that this is not a popular statement, but my responsibility as a teacher of the Scriptures is to tell you the <u>truth</u> as told to us by Christ and the prophets.

Related Verse(s) / Joel 3:13...*Swing the sickle, for the harvest is ripe. Come, trample the grapes, for the winepress is full and the vats overflow—so great is their wickedness!"*

The above verse speaks of the judgments of Jesus being completed. The Wrath of God is coming next, and who in the world could stand that to happen to them? I know this is a bitter pill to accept the fact that there are two different Judgments in The End, but it is clear that Jesus has earned the right to deliver the Seal and Trumpet Judgments, and that Father God will end the process by using the Wrath Judgments coming from the Throne Room.

Looking Forward

The Wrath of God

CHAPTER 15

Seven Angels w/Seven Plagues

We have just read about the Harvesting of the church of Christ. Immediately afterward the Lord avenged those that spit on Him and those who persecuted His church. Those that hurled insults at Jesus while He hung on the cross will soon see the God that they persecuted. It is important to identify what you will be reading in this chapter. What follows is the Wrath of God. This is the same Wrath that Jesus was referring to when speaking to the church at Philadelphia. Please note that as you read through each Wrath of God how many people reversed their standing and asked for mercy and vowed to accept His Son Jesus as their Savior.

Related Verse(s) / Revelation 3:10-11…*Since you have kept my command to endure patiently, I will also keep you from the <u>hour of trial</u> that is going to come upon the whole world to test those who live on the earth.*

<u>***Matthew 24:22***</u>…*If those days had not been cut short, no one would survive, but for the <u>sake of the elect those days will be shortened</u>.*

The elect is the church that will not have to go through the "Hour of Trial" with God being the Judge. The evidence of Jesus has been presented to the world. The time has passed at this point to select Jesus as their Savior.

The church has been harvested and is in the safety of the arms of Christ at this point. The Wrath of God will be raining down on those who rejected Him in just a short time after the Harvest of Believers by Jesus. For the sake of the elect, Jesus will Harvest the Believers before the Wrath of God. The Wrath of God will not be cut short as the last Vial or Bowl judgments announce the end of this world. That is not to say that this Wrath will be prolonged, but that each "Wrath" will be delivered to this earth as scheduled by God long ago. Sometimes many of us forget that God has been the One who has suffered indignities by His chosen people and through the evil ones of this world. God will end all of this degradation directed at His Son and Himself with the Wrath He has warned would be delivered at this time. All the times of choice for mankind will end abruptly when men finally make it clear that they are self-sustaining and do not need God. God will put a stop to grace with mercy and deliver a punishment that will torture men beyond description. There will be no excuses that will make God change His mind. Grace will be taken away from all those who selected Satan over God. Those who rejected God and His Son as being the Creators of this earth will be thrown into the Lake of Burning Sulfur at the Great White Throne Judgment. This punishment will go on forever, a torment without rest. His Wrath will be final and without mercy. Those who will suffer elected to do so by rejecting the Son of God. All those Believers who have accepted Christ as their Savior and followed His commands will escape the Wrath of God.

Related Verse(s) / Romans 1:18- 22...*The wrath of God is being revealed from heaven against all the godlessness and wickedness of men who suppress the truth by their wickedness, since what may be known about God is plain to them, because God has made it plain to them. For since the creation of the world God's invisible qualities—his eternal power and divine nature—have been clearly seen, being understood from what has been made, so that men are without excuse. For although they knew God, they neither glorified him as God nor gave thanks to him, but their thinking became futile and their foolish hearts were darkened Although they claimed to be wise, they became fools and exchanged the glory of the immortal God for images made to look like mortal man and birds and animals and reptiles.*

Read – Chapter 15:1-4

Here the saints who have not received the Mark of the Beast and remained true to the Lord now stand beside Him in heaven. You would think that we should all be in mourning for those who are about to be sentenced to eternal life in the Lake of Burning Sulfur. However, these men and women had the same opportunity we had while living on this earth. We could elect to be with Jesus for eternity, or be with Satan in the pit of hell to be tormented for eternity.

These are the same saints spoken about in Revelation 20:4, who reign with Christ for 1,000 years. The Wrath of God is about to be poured out on the inhabitants of the world. There are no Believers left on earth. Once the Wrath of God begins, there will be no more relief for the unbeliever. There was a celebration going on as we read about the joy over the victory of the saints who went through the Tribulation.

Revelation 20:4-*…I saw thrones on which were seated those who had been given authority to judge. And I saw the souls of those who had been beheaded because of their testimony for Jesus and because of the word of God. They had not worshiped the beast or his image and had not received his mark on their foreheads or their hands. They came to life and reigned with Christ a thousand years.*

These saints will be receiving the reward for living as Believers and remaining loyal to Christ Jesus. It is not an easy thing to do when talking about living for the Lord. Jesus came to earth and experienced what men would do to a man who preached the Gospel. Every family that stands up today and confesses Jesus as Lord of their life will be persecuted in some way; of course, some more serious than others.

Related Verse / Romans 14:11*…It is written: "As surely as I live," says the Lord, "every knee will bow before me; every tongue will confess to God."*

The Holy Spirit will have come home with the church immediately before the Wrath of God. Of course, the record in Revelation showing that no one repented during the Wrath of God confirms that Jesus has drawn back to heaven with his Believers waiting for the Wrath to end.

Related Verse / Revelation 20:2*…He seized the dragon, that ancient serpent, who is the devil, or Satan, and bound him for a thousand years.*

Satan will not see victory ever again. He will have taken all the saints he could when roaming the earth to challenge someone's walk with God. Satan will have fooled one third of those Believers living during the Tribulation. They will not have the knowledge to stand firm and overcome evil. The Dragon has one more shot at the God he hates so much. That will happen shortly after the 1,000 years is over.

We have just read verses concerning the attitude of men as they were receiving their reward for disobedience. We are told again that every knee will bend and all people will bow to the Savior of the world. When looking back on the Seal and Trumpet Judgments we can see the wisdom of reducing the time of these two Judgments. Believers needed the protection of the mark of the Holy Spirit during the judgments of Christ. The Wrath of God does not mention any protection of the saints being needed because they will not be there for this Wrath.

Related Verse(s) / <u>Philippians 2:9-10</u>...*Therefore God exalted him to the highest place and gave him the name that is above every name, <u>that at the name of Jesus every knee should bow,</u> in <u>heaven</u> and on <u>earth and under</u> the earth,*

<u>Read – Chapter 15:5-8</u>

Now the earth is ready for the final Wrath of God. No matter what men of the world did to the Temple of God here on earth, there is a Temple located in heaven that no man can destroy or capture, not even Satan himself. Out of the innermost sacred heart of God comes the most powerful action against this earth that has ever been recorded. This will be worse than the flood experienced in the days of Noah. Although these people will spend eternity in a living hell, they will not die. The pain of death because of the suffering will not be quick during God's Wrath, because death will not come for eternity. In fact, torment will occur every minute of a twenty-four hour cycle, and will continue with a level of torment that is unprecedented in all of history without ever reaching the end of suffering. In life today, pain in our bodies can be controlled by time, that is to say, that time will oftentimes allow the pain to seem less severe and the introduction of pain medicine eases the pain and suffering. However, in the Lake of Burning Sulfur there will be nothing that will ease the torture on the body.

Out of the Temple came the seven angels who will pour out the devastation on what is left of the world. They each received a bowl filled with seven different types of the Wrath of God. The glory of God was so powerful that smoke filled the Temple and it was closed until the Wrath of God was delivered upon the inhabitants left on the earth.

CHAPTER 16

The Wrath of God (Bowls or Vials)

As John looked on, the end of the earth was about to take place. Salvation is over. Death will become something man will desire but will never find. Then men will experience the second death, which puts an end to any creation being left on this earth to deny the power and glory of the Godhead. The Lake of Burning Sulfur will have all of its occupants and the horror and extreme pain for those who rejected God will last forever.

Related Verse(s) / Revelation 6:17...*For the great day of their wrath has come, and who can stand?"*

The two Judgments of Jesus (Seal and Trumpet) have been exposed, and now we will see the final Judgments of Christ and the Wrath of God combined in the end of the world, with an event so excruciating that it will never be seen again. The world as we see it today will be transformed into something that will mirror the Garden of Eden after these events are over.

Read – Chapter 16:1-2

First Bowl or Vial Wrath

The order is given to pour out the First Bowl of the Wrath of God upon the people left on the earth. John saw the people who accepted the "Mark of the Beast" suffer horribly with sores all over their bodies. Remember that we said once a person had taken the Mark of the Beast it was over for them and the mark could not be erased. The mark, once taken, could not be removed. Man's inner feelings of trying to be in control of everything would be his downfall. Situational ethics with man making decisions with only his own vain desires having priority and his determination to reject the Creator of this world will result in assuring a spot in the Lake of Burning Sulfur FOREVER! The one thing they could have done was to acknowledge that Christ Jesus is Lord. Of course, they refused to do that.

Read – Chapter 16:3

Second Bowl or Vial Wrath

This marks the end of all the seas of the world being used for man or beast. Everything in the seas die. People say there is nothing more offensive smelling than that of a decaying body. We can only imagine what that smells like. Combine that with the stench of all sea creatures rotting on top of blood soaked seas, and you have an odor that will permeate the earth.

Read – Chapter 16:4-7

Third Bowl or Vial Wrath

Here John saw all of the available fresh water destroyed by this bowl judgment. The only conceivable fresh water available to these people may be wells they have dug with their hands, although they too may have blood seep into them. There is no escape from the Wrath of God.

We see the Wrath of God is found to be true. The men experiencing these Wraths of God deserve what they are getting. These same men shed the blood of many Christians and prophets of God. God promised that He would take vengeance on all who would persecute us. We were not allowed to take vengeance ourselves. Now, we too can see that the decision to do this was right and we are witnessing the Wrath on those who not only rejected God's Son, but also persecuted and killed many of the saints.

Related Verse(s) / Jeremiah 46:10…*But that day belongs to the Lord, the LORD Almighty—a day of vengeance, for vengeance on his foes.*

Read – Chapter 16:8-9

Fourth Bowl or Vial Wrath

No repentance is found in man even after the sun has increased in intensity to the point where it is searing the skin on man's body. Thank God that He has taken His saints out of the end of this Tribulation Period. He has done what He promised. He has shortened the time of the Tribulation for His saints.

Related Verse(s) / Revelation 3:10…*Since you have kept my command to endure patiently, I will also keep you from the hour of trial that is going to come upon the whole world to test those who live on the earth.*

The intense heat was just a prelude to the Lake of Burning Sulfur these people would have to suffer. To this point, all fresh water had been taken away from those left to suffer. These people were thirsty while also suffering the intense heat from the sun. They had boils all over their bodies. On top of their own skin smelling as if it were burning, these people had to smell the death and destruction of the seas. Is this really what you want to see yourself or your loved-ones go through for eternity? Teach them this study.

Read – Chapter 16:10-11

Fifth Bowl or Vial Wrath

Doesn't this sound a lot like Pharaoh and his people? They too were receiving the Wrath of God and still Pharaoh refused to give up and confess that God was indeed "The God." Millions will not acknowledge that Christ Jesus is Lord and suffer greatly for their rejection.

Here is a group of people who are suffering from the wrath of the sores, who have seen the world's water systems ruined by blood, and then suffered a heat that is so intense that exposure to it burned their skin, yet they refused to acknowledge God. Now they are plunged into darkness where they cannot even see each other. They are part of a world with millions of people in it, yet they cannot see each other, but only hear their screams of pain in the darkness. The pain and loneliness cannot be measured because we know of no such event ever taking place on earth. This Wrath will be carried over to the Lake of Burning Sulfur, and will increase the torment of those who denied Christ.

Those of us living in the mountains across this country can attest to what true darkness really is when the skies are cloudy and there is no light from buildings and streetlights. It is so dark that you cannot see your hand six inches from your face. The momentary feeling can be upsetting. Just imagine this happening around you forever.

Read – Chapter 16:12

Sixth Bowl or Vial Wrath

This is very interesting, not only because of the water drying up, but because it will provide a path to the destruction of those who stand against God. Often mentioned in the Bible are the rivers Euphrates and Tigris. They take a prominent place in end-time prophecy. The valley of Megiddo will be the place where Armageddon will occur.

Read – Chapter 16:13-14

The description given here by John is very disturbing. He saw <u>what looked like</u> frogs coming out of the mouths of the Dragon (Satan), the Antichrist, and the False Prophet. He described them as evil spirits. The only mission of these frog-like creatures is to gather the kings of this world to fight against Christ. To accomplish this they performed many astonishing signs and wonders to encourage the kings to follow them into battle. We will read that the antichrist and the False Prophet will soon be thrown into the Lake of Burning Sulfur.

Read – Chapter 16:15-16

We have to be careful here not to assume that there are still <u>Believers</u> on earth. However, we cannot judge these times with our human thinking. This is a time set aside for the God of this earth to do as He wishes with those left here. The only way we know to God the Father is through His Son Jesus. Without the Holy Spirit to convict men needing Jesus, how will they pass over to a life with Him? Thank God, it is not our call of who goes to heaven and who does not go. My opinion is what I said at the beginning of this chapter. Salvation has slipped away as we see the Holy Spirit returning to heaven with the church.

Christ here is reaffirming to the churches to be ready for the end time events leading up to the Wrath of God. The church of Christ is not being infected with sores, searing skin, launched into total darkness, and left with nothing to drink but blood. The church is in heaven with their Christ. We will read more to reaffirm this as we go along in the text. This is very serious business here. The church has come forth with a way out of having to stand for Christ by escaping the Tribulation by the "Pre- Tribulation Rapture." This is deception at its worst.

Read – Chapter 16:17-21

Seventh Bowl or Vial Wrath

This last bowl judgment results in hailstones weighing over 100 pounds pelting the men of earth. While the tremendous noise is echoing all over the world, islands are sinking into the sea. The mountains of the earth are reduced to flatlands, and the great cities of the world crumpled into unidentifiable piles of rubble. Babylon the Great experiences an extra dose of God's Wrath. Even with all of this, man in his stubbornness cursed God and failed to acknowledge His power.

Here, in this set of verses we read about the fate of the Antichrist and the False Prophet. These two agents of Satan find themselves thrown into the Lake of Burning Sulfur to be tortured for eternity. It is sad to report that Christ will destroy every person alive on this earth, and their souls will be sent to Hades (Hell) to await their final Judgment in the court of God. We already know that they will be sentenced to eternity in the same burning lake as their leaders who deceived them.

Three words mark the end of this earth, as we know it. These words are, "IT IS DONE!" The last earthquake to hit the world comes at this moment. It splits the city of Jerusalem into three parts. Even after all this, men left in this area curse God.

<u>Armageddon</u>

The final dishonor of those who defiled the Lord will be over. Those who thought they could do it their way have found out that God is the only way out of torment. Those who mocked Jesus while He was on the cross and those who made fun of Christians experiencing death, and if not death, disgrace for thousands of years, will be avenged by the Christ of God with His church by His side fulfilling His promise to the church. As God proclaims, "It is Done!," we can read that kings and their armies will meet Jesus and His solders at the place call Armageddon. Jerusalem is split by an earthquake so devastating that the quake stretched over every continent of the world.

Looking Back

Babylon Crushed

• • • ▬▬▬▬▬▬ • ▬▬▬▬▬▬ • • •

CHAPTER 17

The Punishment of the Great Prostitute

Read – Chapter 17:1

Babylon's history of sexual immorality, idol worship, and blatant disrespect for God has made the Lord angry. This city and the people of the world who share its views will experience the total Wrath of God. The reference to the many waters here is the inhabitants of the entire world who are of one mind with the evil motives of this city. The following prophecy from Jeremiah tells of its demise.

> **Related Verse(s)** / Jeremiah 51:6-9…*"Flee from Babylon! Run for your lives! Do not be destroyed because of her sins. It is time for the LORD's vengeance; he will pay her what she deserves. Babylon was a gold cup in the LORD's hand; she made the whole earth drunk. The nations drank her wine; therefore they have now gone mad. Babylon will suddenly fall and be broken. Wail over her! Get balm for her pain; perhaps she can be healed. "'We would have healed Babylon, but she cannot be healed; let us leave her and each go to his own land, for her judgment reaches to the skies, it rises as high as the clouds.'*

Look at why Babylon is responsible to the Lord for her actions. It was bad enough that she was a city of evil, but she spread that evil to other countries and especially to God's chosen people, as they were taken captive there for 70 years. The evil that came out of Babylon could not be reversed unless men would see the evil of their ways and turn to Jesus.

Read – Chapter 17:2

There is always a price to pay for disobedience to the Creator of the world. God's memory is not affected by age. If the people of the world attack and hurt the children of God, they will pay the ultimate price for their aggression by spending eternity in the Lake of Burning Sulfur.

Kingship carries with it the false sense of invincibility. No king wants to give up his kingdom to another king. Even though Christ Jesus offers kings the same opportunity that you and I have to accept Him and live better than a king in eternity, they just cannot give up the counterfeit power they have. The price these kings will pay is death in the Great War they have been appointed to conduct. In your reading of the description of Babylon, see if another nation comes to mind. Can you think of a nation who has done its best to drive God out of its government and has the morals today of ancient Babylon? Sure you can, it is the United States!

Read – Chapter 17:3-5

MYSTERY *BABYLON THE GREAT* THE MOTHER OF PROSTITUTES AND OF THE ABOMINATIONS OF THE EARTH

When people become indignant to authority, they become very emboldened in their attitudes. In this case, they have become so evil that they taught others to accept evil as a position deserving tribute. Their boldness turned into brash stupidity as they taunted their Creator with the filthiness of their actions. These people became poster children for Satan. They worked against God in the world courts. They blaspheme God and try to get His name removed from every document in the world. They proudly display their sin before the peoples of the earth, and try to recruit them to their cause. This is the time that has been reserved for them to experience the Wrath of God. Take heed people of this world. God cannot be destroyed. He is alive and will soon deliver the Wrath talked about in the book of Revelation. Let all men understand that God cannot be mocked without penalty.

Related Verses / Galatians 6:7-8…*Do not be deceived: **God cannot be mocked**. A man reaps what he sows. The one who sows to please his* *sinful nature, from that nature will reap destruction; the one who sows to please the Spirit, from the Spirit will reap eternal life.*

Read – Chapter 17:6-8

So many Believers have been victimized by the mindset of Babylon. Persecution and death to the saints of God have been rampant during this time, and of course before the Great Tribulation. Thousands upon thousands of missionaries and Believers around the world have been killed for their witness of Christ and their valiant fight against the wickedness of the world.

The Beast the people will support is the antichrist. He was once here on earth. He suffered a fatal head wound and then would return to live again as the antichrist. He came to life again and the people of our world will accept him as a savior of sort. He will be a hero by saving the economy of the world. The truth is that he rises out of the ashes of the Abyss, and begins to rule as the Tribulation begins. You should know that the Abyss is "home base" for the evil trinity. The antichrist, with the blessing of Satan, will eventually rule over the people of the world. The False Prophet will receive a blessing from the antichrist to enforce Satan's rules. Both will astonish the people of the world with wonders and signs to the point where most people will think that the antichrist is really the Christ of God.

The inhabitants of the earth whose names have not been written in the Book of Life from the creation of the world will be astonished when they see the Beast, because he once was, now is not, and yet will come.

Related Verse / Revelation 17:8…The beast, which you saw, once was, now is not, and will come up out of the Abyss and go to his destruction.

Daniel 7:25…He will speak against the Most High and oppress his saints and <u>try to change</u> the set times and the laws.

The antichrist will appear again to the mass of humanity alive and well with a mark on his head of the fatal wound he has suffered. You will remember that Christ Jesus was crucified, died, and buried. He was then brought out of the grave by His Father resulting in victory over death. Jesus showed His wounds of that experience to the Apostle Thomas to prove to all that He was indeed the same Christ. The antichrist mimicked Christ in that he had a wound on his head that appeared to be a result of death. However, he will come back from the dead and try to take the position of the real Christ of God.

Do not forget about the evil authority that Satan has given over to the Beast. The Beast will be thrown into the Lake of Burning Sulfur as will Satan when the time is right. We will read that Satan will return to the Abyss for 1,000 years and then come back to be defeated by the breath of God.

Read – Chapter 17:9-11

We have to look at this very carefully because it is very easy to interpret this in error. I think it would be helpful if we look back on the last few empires that have threatened or subdued the Israelites. Egypt is one of the empires that tried to reduce or destroy the Israeli population. Remember, they had all the male babies killed because they were becoming more populous than the Egyptians (Exodus 1:15-16). The Assyrian army defeated the armies of Judah and Israel with the blessing of God. Babylon most certainly could be among those who looked for the destruction of Jerusalem and the tribes of the Nation of Israel turning them into a nation that abandoned Father God and worshiped all of their false gods. All of these cities mentioned were considered the prostitute city of their time. Persia is another empire seeking the destruction of the Jews. We read about this empire in the book of Esther where the Jews came close to being destroyed because of a man named Haman. The city of Persepolis was the prostitute city of that era. The Seleucid Empire forbade the practicing of Judaism and desecrated the temple in Jerusalem. The prostitute city of this empire was Antioch. Of course there are many more.

Another to be considered is the prostitute city of Rome. The Roman Empire was no friend to the Jew and was responsible in part for killing Christ Jesus. Although Rome does not play a dominate role in the world today, it is getting ready to reestablish its role in the domination of the world's economy. It is possible that the antichrist will come out of Rome. Today, Italy is getting into a severe financial crisis and the people of this country will be very open to a man, who comes on the scene, with all the answers to solving their problems. Once Italy is seen as recovering well after their financial crisis, other countries will be interested in what the new leader of Italy has to say. It will happen very quickly as the television networks give us an hour by hour picture of the promised antichrist.

Read – Chapter 17:12-14

Ten kingdoms or countries will share in the war against the Lamb of God. We have now in our world today ten kingdoms that are willing and yearn for the destruction of Israel. Several surround the country of Israel right now. When we look at the countries that surround or are near Israel it is not difficult to find more Arab countries that would fight to destroy the Jews.

Read – Chapter 17:15-18

So we can say in summary that many peoples of the world who think they have a pact with the new evil will be destroyed by that same evil. God has given this beast to exercise power over man and will withdraw that power and throw him into the Lake of Burning Sulfur, along with the False Prophet and soon after that, Satan himself.

CHAPTER 18

The End of Evil in Babylon

Read – Chapter 18:1-3

Here we see another angel that has great authority. The power of this angel illuminated the earth. God honored many angels for not being deceived by Satan. The splendor of this angel was magnificent. He spoke with a voice of authority as he shouted the evil done by the people of this city.

Could it be that God is so angry at a city because its king conquered Jerusalem? Or, could it be that in addition to being conquered, God's people took on the sins of the conqueror? Think about it. The nation, that is the twelve tribes that crossed the Jordan River to take the "Promised Land," never did assemble again as a nation under God until 1948. After the defeat and downfall of Jerusalem in 70 A.D., the Jewish Nation filtered into other societies taking on their customs and practices. It is important to understand that the Jewish nation also took the culture and customs of Babylon back with them. Christ identified Babylon as the center of evil. Of course, those who were residents in that city and those who learned to love evil from her, do not look upon the evil of Babylon as a reason for the Wrath of God. These people believe that they are in complete control of their lives and the land they live in. Does this sound like another country whose people believe they deserve unabated freedom without consequences? There is a price to pay for disobedience.

God warned Babylon repeatedly to change her ways and accept the Creator of this world. However, when people are enjoying doing what excites them, nothing can change their minds concerning their behavior. To most people at that time, Babylon represented the freedom that allows people to do whatever their reprobate minds lead them to do. Babylon today describes many cities of the world, including many cities in the United States. It is difficult to read about this city that was abolished long ago, yet God's memory is everlasting when His people are mistreated and misled. God does indeed get the last word.

In the time of Pharaoh, the nation of Israel, although under great persecution, remained together with a common cause and recognized the Lord of creation as their God. Since the destruction of the temple and the capture of the people of Jerusalem by Nebuchadnezzar in 586 B.C., the nation has never been the same in unity or spirit until 1948. The separation from their Messiah caused them to be cursed by God and it would be a long time before their eyes would be opened again to who their Savior is.

Related Verse(s) / <u>Isaiah 56:10-11</u>…*<u>Israel's watchmen</u> are <u>blind, they all lack knowledge</u>; they are all mute dogs, they cannot bark; they lie around and dream, they love to sleep. They are dogs with mighty appetites; they never have enough. They <u>are shepherds who lack understanding</u>; they all turn to their own way, each seeks his own gain.*

<u>Read – Chapter 18:4-8</u>

Next, we hear a voice coming from heaven pleading with the Jews to leave this city. They were asked not to take anything that was given to them by their captors or anything they earned that would be considered sinful. The voice from heaven once again called down fire on the city of Babylon. The torment of this will be so horrific that the kings of the world will tremble as they watch the demise of their cities.

Related Verse(s) / <u>Ezekiel 43:1-2</u>…*Then the man brought me to the gate facing east, and I saw the glory of the God of Israel coming from the east.*

His voice was like the roar of rushing waters, and the land was radiant with his glory.

Isaiah 48:20...*Leave Babylon, flee from the Babylonians! Announce this with shouts of joy and proclaim it. Send it out to the ends of the earth; say, "The LORD has redeemed his servant Jacob."*

Here the Scripture is screaming out to us to back out of the sin caused by being an active participant in the actions of people who represent the evil of Babylon. Our Babylon is the unrepentant city or area in which we live. Our cities, states, and country have reversed themselves on issues that are important to God and His people. We are doing all we can to push God completely out of our lives. The line between Christian and sinner has been so blurred that it is barely visible anymore. Now we have to rely even more on the Holy Spirit for guidance through even the simplest of life's paths. And yet we do not find the Holy Spirit being accepted in many of our churches.

Can you see the picture of what Babylon represents to our Lord? Is it unreasonable for God to have a feeling of disdain for the city of Babylon and so many more as bad or worse around the world? To have so many chapters in the Revelation of the Christ devoted to telling us of the destruction of this city, and all those who would take part in the same evil, should make us tremble. Many of us have lived, or are now living, in cities that make Babylon seem like a sweet country town. There should be a real sense of guilt in the personal actions of those populations that ignore consequences for their evil behavior.

Read – Chapter 18:9-10

Kings of the earth will weep because they understand that the same thing will happen to them. Those who are still engrossed in sin today should look at this example, and ask God for forgiveness and accept Salvation through His Son.

Related Verse(s) / Romans 10:9...*That if you confess with your mouth, "Jesus is Lord," and believe in your heart that God raised him from the dead, you will be saved.*

Read – Chapter 18:11-13

As the end of this world is drawing to the climax of total destruction, merchants of the world will weep and mourn over her. Carbon copies of Babylon will no longer be cities in which men will stop over and participate in the immoral behavior on the streets of evil. Look at what men were looking for in these cities; not only selling and buying of goods and services, but also looking to engage in the evil of a society filled with immorality. It also meant that they were supporting false gods that accepted babies as sacrifices.

Babylon was destroyed as a city and a state long ago, but the evil effects of this city's social life would carry on right up until this very day. We are reading about the final destruction of carbon copy Babylon as part of the "end" of this world and the evil it represents. Finally, abhorrent behavior is not acceptable any more. As we look around us today we see people who are on edge because of the world's economy. God plays a role in society today. He once served as our God and our spiritual leader. We recognized Him as the Creator of this world and all the people. Now, God appears to many to be a little old man without any power and unable to deliver any consequences to those who have denied Him. The description of God's power in these verses does not sound like they are from a weak old man, but from a powerful God who has been treated like a sick old creature. Serious punishment will be given to those who deny Him and His Son Jesus. The torment that these people will live through will be torture without end for eternity.

Read – Chapter 18:14-17

What will happen to these cities? Now people who once could not wait to reach these carbon copy cities like Babylon will scramble for the countryside in fear. Those that can will try to keep a safe distance so they would not have to suffer the pain and torment of evil. The sounds of weeping and screaming within their cities will tremble as they experience the destruction of the cities they loved.

The chronicles record that in just one hour, sixty minutes, the city of Babylon was laid waste. Captains of ships withdrew their vessels from the ports to avert the destruction that was happening as they watched this city disintegrate. Of course we are seeing this as an event that has already happened in the course of the timing of the Tribulation. We are seeing the final wrath that will be given to evil cities that represent the evil of Babylon.

Read – Chapter 18:18-19

The capitol of sin was falling apart and many were crying to watch such a sight. An example of how people will feel when looking at the destruction will be the same as if we here in the United States were watching a city like New York City go through the destruction described here concerning Babylon. Yet New York City is one that would make Babylon look like a novice when it comes to perverse living. This event could indeed be the city of New York, Los Angeles, San Francisco, etc. and no doubt will suffer the same destruction as Babylon.

As we read about this destruction, how many people do we read are getting down on their knees, and asking God for forgiveness of their sins? The answer, of course, is zero. In fact, we read that they threw dust over their heads, which is a sign of mourning, and are still in shock that a city of wealth and of this size could be leveled in just one hour.

Read – Chapter 18:20-21

Finally, justice will be administered to those who persecuted the saints of the Lord and spit on the name of God and His Son. An angel from heaven gives us an example of how the evil cities like Babylon will be reduced to nothing. These cities will never again have the opportunity to lead so many people away from God.

Never again will music come from cities like this one. Never again will we hear a city worker making noise in the city. The sounds of trade in agriculture and others will be silenced. Darkness will overcome the city and the sounds of happiness and pleasure will fade away never to be heard from again.

The spell that had been cast over all who entered the city will be broken. The lure of evil in cities such as Las Vegas, Reno, and Atlantic City are gone and what replaces that lure is total destruction. As we look into these evil cities like Babylon after its destruction, we see that the blood of all the saints of the earth lay in the city center. Can you understand now why God hated cities like these and wanted to destroy them with His Wrath? I understand that much of this is overwhelming as you read these words. We must understand that there is a price to pay for the disobedience of man as the world nears the end of its existence.

All that we can acquire through life; wealth, power, prestige, and greatness can be taken away in a whisper of time. In our day, a nation may have a healthy supply of wealth and power due to oil production, but can be a nation of paupers in just a few minutes of overwhelming military force. Woe to the city that has turned its back on God and has perverted the world by its behavior.

There is a time when those who have been persecuted for the name of Christ will see the reward for their obedience. One of those rewards will be seeing the destruction of evil. Destruction here is final! There will be no traces of evil when Christ Jesus, after 1,000 years, delivers with Father God a New Heaven and a New Earth. In fact, the earth that will continue for the Millennium has to be transformed into its original state. Those who reside on earth during the Millennium will see an earth without the damage done to it as the people of our time have decimated their land. It will not be a new earth; that will happen at the end of the Millennium as God replaces the old with the new, both heaven and earth.

The Future

The Second Coming of Christ

Chapter 19

CHAPTER 19

The Second Coming of Christ

John is still looking at the smoking ruins of the demolished Babylon. The dark cloud of smoke can be seen around the world.

Read – Chapter 19:1-3

These verses are saying that this perverse city will be thrown into the Lake of Burning Sulfur, which is the second death, only to live eternally with overwhelming torment and loneliness. The Lake of Burning Sulfur will be the new eternal home for those people responsible for the corruption of the world and the refusal of billions of people to accept Jesus as the Son of God.

Sulfur gives off a suffocating smell. This odor will leave a person gasping for breath. In this case, in the Lake of Burning Sulfur, gasping for breath will not stop for even one second and will last forever. All those who reject Christ will spend eternity in this horrible burning lake.

Something else was about to happen. You can feel that just by reading the verses here. We are about to hear from the twenty-four elders and the four creatures in the Throne Room of God. A celebration that will last forever can be heard throughout the heavens. Both you and I will have a part in this celebration.

<u>***Read – Chapter 19:4-8***</u>

<u>The Wedding Supper of the Lamb</u>

The destruction of Babylon has been completed. All of the nations have been given the last opportunity to accept Christ at the sound of the last Trumpet Judgment by our Savior. The only thing left was to do battle against the evil of the world, and evil will lose that battle.

Next, the bride of Christ (His Church) will come to seal the covenant of spending eternity with Him. The celebration will no doubt be one like the wedding of those who love each other and are willing to serve each other without reservation forever. We have been waiting for this moment for a long time. Forever, which seems like the time it has taken to reach eternity with the Lord, is now here. All of the past troubles and fears are erased. We will complete our supper with the Lamb of God and then live in a place that words cannot express the wonderment contained in it. All pain will be gone and only comfort and joy will prevail. Politics, gossip, and judging will be over forever. We will be with our Savior for eternity.

Related Verse(s) / Luke 14:15…*When one of those at the table with him heard this, he said to Jesus, "Blessed is the man who will eat at the feast in the kingdom of God."*

The saints will be equipped with their heavenly bodies, sanctified, and robed in white ready to be a part of the Lord's army. We will sit down with Him as a bride sits with her husband on their wedding day. In this case, it took many years of persecution, many years of troubles for the bride, and trillions of tears shed by His followers, but now those days of suffering are over. Never again will we see pain, tears, or anxiety as a function of our minds or bodies.

Related Verse: / <u>Revelation 21:4</u>…*He will wipe every tear from their eyes. There will be no more death or mourning or crying or pain, for the old order of things has passed away."*

<u>***Read – Chapter 19:9-10***</u>

Worshiping Christ will now take on a new understanding of all Jesus did for us as we enter a new dimension, forgetting the past and looking forward. We now will prepare to go to war supporting Jesus. Just as it was in our earthly life with Christ, defeating our enemies, so it will be in this fight. With just the words that come out of His mouth, the enemy will die. Those who doubted the words of Christ concerning the end will face death and torment.

The wedding supper of the Lamb is by invitation only. The invitation was given as an open ended invitation. Anyone could send an RSVP to Father God by accepting the Son of God as his or her Lord and Savior.

Saying the words of accepting Jesus for who He is and then living for Him will mean that there is a seat with your name on it in heaven. No introductions will have to be made because we will all be family.

Read – Chapter 19:11-16

KING OF KINGS AND LORD OF LORDS

Finally, God is about to pour out His total and final wrath on the people who have rejected him. There will be no more phony miracles from the Beast and the False Prophet. The time has come for the world to understand that God has the power to create and to destroy.

Read – Chapter 19:17-18

Great Supper of God

One of the last orders given out to an angel in heaven is to call every bird in the air to come for a final feast. This supper marks the end of mankind until we reach the final destruction by God as Satan is released for a time to gather the kings of the earth. The birds will be gorging themselves on every single person and animal left on this planet. The great supper of God closes out the book on the creation of man as we look on to the Millennium.

Related Verse: / *Mark 10::33…"We are going up to Jerusalem," he said, "and the Son of Man will be betrayed to the chief priests and teachers of the law. They will condemn him to death and will hand him over to the Gentiles, who will mock him and <u>spit on him</u>, flog him and kill him. Three days later he will rise."*

Those who thought going to church was just for hypocrites now stand in horror of what is ahead for them. It will be a sad thing if any of our family is included in this group deserving hell. It is our responsibility to inform them that Jesus wants to save them from this moment. We must tell them. The final decision is theirs, if we do not tell them who will?

Read – Chapter 19:19-21

The Beast (antichrist) and the False Prophet will be thrown alive into the Lake of Burning Sulfur, and be there for eternity; tormented day and night; 24 hours per day, every day, and forever! As both of these men were ruling the world, they showed their strength and power by calling fire down from heaven. They performed many miracles. The people of the world were amazed for the first three and a half years of their existence. Then the False Prophet began to demand that everyone take the Mark of the Beast for banking needs. Just as they thought that they were in control, they were tossed into the Burning Sulfur. Their armies became food for the birds of the air as they fell and ended up being the great supper of God. I know these sounds awful, but there is a price to pay for the rejection of the God of this world.

The relationship that God originally intended for man and Himself was to walk in the cool of the evening enjoying each other's company. The human race will be given blessings beyond description. The waiting is over now, and we the church will spend forever together with the God we love and live for today.

The Millennium Covenant

Chapter 20

CHAPTER 20

The Millennium Covenant

Read – Chapter 20:1-3

There have been many angels used by God to accomplish different tasks that were associated with "End Times". The angel we are now reading about is soon to throw Satan into the Abyss and chain him up for one thousand years. Please note that Satan is bound in the Abyss with the fallen angels who, like Satan, stood against God and were sentenced to the Abyss until they, like all who reject God, will spend eternity in the Burning Lake of Sulfur. Now we have an angel from heaven with the power to subdue the powerful Satan and chain him up for many earthly lifetimes. All the power that has been bragged about by Satan; and here we see an angel take power over him. What would make Satan think he could ever defeat the power of God? We all know what that was. It had to be his pride. At one time, he was the most beautiful angel in all of heaven. Because he was the most beautiful angel and had the ear of God, he thought that he could replace God and reach a level above the LORD just by his own power. In Satan's mind's eye, he could see the Creator of the world bowing down to him.

Here we read the false pride of Satan as he boasts while in heaven that he will have a throne above the God of heaven. We know how that turns out.

Related Verse(s) / Isaiah 14:12-15...*How you have fallen from heaven, O morning star, son of the dawn! You have been cast down to the* *earth, you who once laid low the nations! You said in your heart, "I will ascend to heaven; I will raise my throne above the stars of God; I will sit enthroned on the mount of assembly, on the utmost heights of the sacred mountain. I will ascend above the tops of the clouds; I will make myself like the Most High." But <u>you are brought down</u> to the grave, <u>to the depths of the pit</u>.*

Related Verse(s) / <u>Luke 10:18</u>…*Jesus replied, "I saw <u>Satan fall like lightning</u> from heaven. I have given you authority to trample on snakes and scorpions and to overcome all the power of the enemy; nothing will harm you. However, do not rejoice that the spirits submit to you, but rejoice that your names are written in heaven."*

Here we see where the real power lies. If Jesus can make the demons of this world submit to our commands through His name, we can see that Satan's power is shallow and impotent against us because Christ lives in us. This will be very critical to remember as time draws nearer to the Birth Pains just before the Tribulation period.

After being bound for a thousand years, Satan will be released for a short time by God. Satan could have stayed in the Abyss forever, but God set up a special place for those, including Satan, who would defy the words of Christ. The Lake of Burning Sulfur waits for Satan as well. Satan will have no relief in the Lake of Burning Sulfur. He will not have a path to speak with God, but he will suffer just like those who followed him. Victory may seem close, but God is always the Victor and will be for eternity. It would be wise for all to understand that truism.

<u>Read – Chapter 20:4-5</u>

In verse four, we see that there are people to judge at the beginning of the Millennium. We also see that only those who have lost their lives standing up for Jesus will judge with Him. Then we read probably the most important words when it comes to end time prophecy. <u>This is the First Resurrection!</u> The <u>Second Resurrection</u> will not happen until after the Millennium is over. This piece of Scripture is often overlooked by those who attempt to convince us of an early coming of Christ.

What does it mean when the text says, "they came to life?" Does that mean they were dead? If so, where were they? They were certainly not left in the grave. Remember the two places I explained that were created for those who die prior to the end of the world? Those two places are Hades and Paradise. Those who die without accepting Jesus as the Christ of God will be held for judgment in Hades. The second place was the Paradise of God. Jesus mentioned it as He was dying on the cross when He said to a convict being crucified with Him, *"today you will be with me in Paradise"* (Luke 23:43). He immediately went to Paradise when he took his last breath here on earth. The same thing happens to those of us who have given our lives over to Jesus and follow His commands. There is another place where the family of God is held, and that is under the altar of God. These Believers are those who will be beheaded during the Tribulation, and earn a special place of honor with Christ. They will rule with Christ over those who will be in the Millennium.

Revelation 2:7-8...*He who has an ear, let him hear what the Spirit says to the churches. To <u>him who overcomes</u>, I will give the right to eat from the tree of life, which is <u>in the paradise of God</u>.*

Revelation 6:9...*When he opened the fifth seal, I saw under the altar the souls of those who had been slain because of the word of God and the testimony they had maintained.*

Read – Chapter 20:6

Doesn't this sound exactly like what God would do for those who have gone through the fire of persecution? Listen for a moment. Those of us who die before the Tribulation are with Jesus instantly after our last breath on earth. Our next breath is taken in the Paradise of the Lord. We are already with God in His Paradise when the Tribulation begins. We just don't lay in the grave waiting for some sort of rapture event to happen. We are already enjoying the benefits of heaven for eternity. We will take on our new heavenly body when we take the next breath after death here on earth. We will indeed meet those who are still alive and meet them in the air when Jesus gathers all the saints.

Related Verse(s) / Romans 8:30...*And those he predestined, he also called; those he called, <u>he also justified</u>; those he justified, <u>he also glorified</u>.*

Read – Chapter 20:7-10

The Last Battle

This short time encompasses an event that is only described here in this chapter of Revelation. Satan will gather the people left on this earth from all nations and move to surround the city of Jerusalem. Kings and Queens will gather to fight the last battle with God, except there is no battle. Once they have gathered around Jerusalem, fire will come down from heaven and destroy them all! Please do not confuse this with any other battle described in the book of Revelation. This event will happen very quickly and Satan will join the antichrist and the False Prophet in the Lake of Burning Sulfur to be tormented for eternity, as the Great White Throne Judgment had begun.

Read – Chapter 20:11

The picture here is of a people who cannot hide from the judgment of God. The judgment of the world begins. ALL men and women will account for their lives while here on earth. All of a sudden, this event that men and women scoffed at when they were alive is now a reality.

There is no place to hide, as every soul will have to be accountable to Christ. All that every man has done will be exposed for judgment. The Book of Life is the same book that was used to allow you to be harvested as a saint of Christ immediately after the last trumpet judgment. This Book of Life contains all the names of those men and women who lived for the Lord. It is important to remember that Believers before this have been adjudicated free from sin as they enter the rest of God as they were harvested after the last trumpet of Christ. The proof of that statement is found in Romans 6:22 / Hebrews 4:10. No person who had any sin in their life would be able to sit at the table of the Wedding Supper of the Lamb.

Read – Chapter 20:12

Let's discuss our lives today. Your life is being recorded as we speak. The important thing to remember is that if your name is recorded in the Book of Life, all of the sin you were responsible for has been erased. We will have to give an account of our Christian life at the timing of Christ, but it will not be for guilt or innocence of sin. There will be no excuses, no back talk, no trying to convince Christ to overlook our sin. Anyone whose name is not written in the Book of Life will be thrown into the same Lake of Burning Sulfur as Satan. There will be no arguments about whose name deserves to be written in this book. There were commands of God and of His Son Christ Jesus that all people should have followed. If your name is not found in this book, you will spend eternity in the Lake of Burning Sulfur to be tormented forever with no rest. The same is true of those who have gone through the Millennium. Obedience pays big dividends as we stand in front of God.

Revelation 3:5...*He who <u>overcomes will</u>, like them, be dressed in white. I will <u>never blot out his name from the book of life</u>, but will acknowledge his name before my Father and his angels.*

Read – Chapter 20:13-15

No one can escape the judgment of Christ. It doesn't make any difference whether the person died at sea and was never recovered, or had been cremated so they were turned to dust. <u>All</u> will stand with an open book of our lives in front of God.

The second death is a sentence of eternal life in the Lake of Burning Sulfur where everyone in it will be tormented beyond imagination. Who would be so ignorant to turn away from God and His Son, and pick eternal life in torment?

Finally, all mankind has been judged and there is no one left on this earth. There is no heaven or earth, as we know it by this time. It is all over! Man Has Seen The Final Eclipse.

Eternal Life

———⋅•◦●◦•⋅————⋅●⋅————⋅•◦●◦•⋅———

CHAPTER 21

The New Jerusalem

Read – Chapter 21:1

Something huge is beginning to happen. As we are standing in heaven looking toward earth, a city that looks like it is covered with gem stones of all kinds is coming to rest on a New Earth. While we are looking at this New City covered with every gemstone that we can think of coming to rest on a New Earth, the memory of the last event in Chapter Twenty is fading out of remembrance. Just like there will be no need for the light of the sun and moon, so there will be no need for seas. Everything we need for a heavenly survival for eternity will be supplied by God. The glory of God will be all the light we will need.

    Revelation 21:2-3…*I saw the Holy City, the new Jerusalem, coming down out of heaven from God, prepared as a bride beautifully dressed for her husband. And I heard a loud voice from the throne saying, "Now the dwelling of God is with men, and he will live with them. They will be his people, and God himself will be with them and be their God.*

Read – Chapter 21:2-5

    Most of us have seen the current city of Jerusalem by television reports coming from that area. At the appointed time, we will see a brand new city coming down from heaven. This city was being prepared for us since the beginning of time. As we enter this New Earth and New

Heaven, we must be able to feel the glory of God resting on us. God will join His Son in living with us. Do you really understand what a great and awesome thing that will be? There will be no more pain and suffering. In fact, we will experience a brand new way of life. A new earth, a new city, and a new life are the rewards for being obedient to the Son of God, Christ Jesus.

Can you remember what the smell of a new car was like after buying the vehicle? You may also remember a trip through the woods and a stream that trickled down to a small gathering point. Not only will we be bedazzled by the New Jerusalem, we will be entranced by the wonderful smell of nature. It will be a thousand times better than the smell we experienced in the car or the forest.

Millions of people will enjoy a relationship with the true God as their Father. For the first time in their lives, they will feel a closeness that has eluded them for all the years they were on this earth, yet they held on and overcame persecution and doubt. We will see God for who He really is and experience His love as He wipes away the last tears left in the world. Death had been defeated by the Son of God, which has allowed us to defeat the same foe. We knew we could not fight what would be sent against us in the beginning of the Tribulation. Now we can truly say that without the love of Christ and His Father, we would be lost forever in sin.

Read – Chapter 21:6-8

The end has come! The One who was, and is, and will be forever has closed the book on the story of the created earth. This book will never be opened again. The reason is that it would cause pain that would be too much to handle. Listen to God reaching out to those who do not know Him. As He spreads out His hand over the New Jerusalem and the New Earth it sits on, He will tell everyone that this is a free gift to them for believing in His Son Jesus.

Look at those who stand no chance of seeing what we are talking about in this chapter. Those who are cowards, unbelievers, vile, murderers, sexually immoral, seers, idolaters, and all liars are going to die the second death. All they would have to do is to ask Jesus for the life- giving water through forgiveness and restoration, but they will refuse and consequently find themselves in a Lake of Burning Sulfur for eternity.

Right here in the middle of all this awe and wonder, I would like to inject a little reality of what it took Believers to get to this point. If a survey was taken in the year of 2010 of who thought they were going to heaven, the numbers would be high for those saying, yes, I will go to heaven. But what if you were told a lie saying that you would not have to experience any pain and suffering in the Tribulation Period? After being promised that by your spiritual leaders, and then being tricked by a man posing as Christ who came along and with a few counterfeit miracles convinced you to follow him, how will you feel as you stand before Christ with the Mark of the Beast? That, of course, will assure that you will spend eternity in the Lake of Burning Sulfur.

May God have mercy on those who continue to deceive the masses about a Pre-Tribulation Rapture. There is a price to pay for religious leaders defrauding their congregations. Many of these leaders honestly believe the message they are giving, but the Bible says that we who lead are held to a higher standard. We as pastors must be exceedingly careful when we speak of the return of our Savior.

Related Verse(s) / James 3:1…*Not many of you should presume to be teachers, my brothers, because you know that we who teach will be judged more strictly.*

Revelation 21:7… *He who overcomes will inherit all this, and I will be his God and he will be my son.*

Now, take note of what God is saying to John. Jesus says, "*He who overcomes will inherit all this, and I will be his God and he will be my son.*" Ladies and gentlemen, you must be prepared to overcome any persecution that this world can throw at you. Don't let some well-meaning false prophet, pastor, minister, priest, elder, or bishop come along and convince you that you are too good and God is too kind to allow you to be persecuted. Men and women of Christ have been persecuted since the first message of Jesus. What do they say when they are reminded of hundreds of thousands of Christians being beheaded and killed for the name of Christ in the Sudan for example? Those Christians being persecuted and killed for the name of Christ will never accept the theory that God would not allow His people to suffer. The only thing they hold on to is the promise that God made to them that they will be overcomers!

Read – Chapter 21:9-14

How could I write anything more wonderful in giving you a picture of your future home? John looked at the great city of God. Its gates were representative of the Twelve Tribes of Israel. The foundation was twelve layers representing the apostles of the Christ Himself.

Read – Chapter 21:15-21

This city is measured as 1,400 miles wide, 1,400 miles long and 1,400 miles high. It is a perfect cube. The thickness of the walls was about 200 feet. I have been told that a city of this size could hold millions of people, all in their own living quarters.

Read – Chapter 21:22-27

Here the word of God tells us that the Father and the Son will illuminate this new world. Some will live outside the city, but its gates will never be closed, and the light of God will shine forever.

We get a short glimpse into how the new world will operate when we read verses 24 through 27. *"On no day will its gates ever be shut, for there will be no night there. The glory and honor of the nations will be brought into it."*

The nations of the world are those that will be established in the new transformed eternal life. *"Nothing impure will ever enter it, nor will anyone who does what is shameful or deceitful, but only those whose names are written in the Lamb's book of life."* All the population of the newly transformed world will be Born-Again Believers. Gates of cities are meant for going in and out, and the New Jerusalem will be no different. I look forward to meeting you there.

CHAPTER 22

Comfort & Warning

Read – Chapter 22:1-5

Although there is no sea, there is a river flowing through the city containing the water of life. We know that time will be measured in at least months, because the two Trees of Life will bear different fruit each month. The leaves of the trees represent healthy nations as robust as the leaves on these special trees.

The curse has been removed from the Garden of Eden and from man. The conditions on this new earth must look like a huge Garden of Eden. We will walk with God and have fellowship with Him. Isn't that what He wanted from the very beginning?

Read – Chapter 22:6

John has now seen the evolution of the plan of God for His people. He has seen what no man has seen before, or will ever see again until we are at home with the Lord with a new earth and a new heaven. John will live out the rest of his life with the pictures in his mind of both the torment of men and the glory of God. This had to be exciting for him as well as giving him a new mission to tell all those he could speak to about the end of this world.

Now it is up to us to take what He has given us and use it to prepare for the time when we have to overcome persecution. Be very careful not to be led astray by those who will tell you that there is some sort of an event that will take you up to see Jesus in the air prior to The Great Tribulation. Jesus does not sneak back to an earth He created and then slither back to heaven. This is His earth, we are His creation, and He will never be afraid to approach what He created!

Read – Chapter 22:7-9

We MUST hold up the Godhead of Heaven who created us and put God back on His throne. John is now repeating the blessing offered by Christ Jesus at the beginning of this book. Listen and do what you are asked to do. Worship God! As we see the end of this old world being changed into something that has to be comparable to the Garden of Eden, we must take heart. God has done what He said He would do and that is giving us a mansion to live in and a God that will never leave us for eternity.

Read – Chapter 22:10-11

Both sinner and saint have the opportunity to hear what the Son of God says. We still have the choice to accept the Salvation that Christ Jesus has to offer. That chance ends when we take our last breath here on earth. If you have been following the story of the end of the earth, you no doubt have come to a crisis in your life. Either you believe everything Jesus has said in the book of Revelation or you have a crisis of belief. If you have doubts, please continue to study the Revelation of Christ Jesus. The Holy Spirit will make truth become evident to you as you give your heart over to His leading.

Read – Chapter 22:12

The final authority is Jesus, the only Christ of God, and we must know all we can about Him, and be ready for Him when He calls us home. We put a lot of effort into trying to understand the timing of His coming. Those efforts are important, but understand this: your "end time" on this earth will probably come by disease or accident. You must be ready to stand in front of Christ at any moment. If you are not ready to meet Jesus right this very moment, it is safe to say that should you have to be exposed to persecution, you will fail miserably. That thought should be extremely sobering. I understand that life is more complicated than it was years ago, but we serve the same great God whose love has remained and who is prepared to extend that love to us regardless of how awful the circumstances of our past life.

Read – Chapter 22:14-16

Because you have accepted Jesus as your Savior, you have the right to partake of the Trees of Life that stands on either side of the river flowing from the Throne of God. Blessed are we who have given our life over to Jesus. We will receive the pure white robes when we leave this world. We become a resident of the New Jerusalem the minute we receive Christ. Today sin is all around us, yet we will be given our reward in the timing of God.

Read – Chapter 22:17

If you do not know Christ as your personal Savior, this may be your last opportunity to accept Him. It is totally your choice. Why would anyone turn down the opportunity to live with God for eternity, when the other option would be selecting living in the Lake of Burning Sulfur with Satan for all eternity?

The Revelation of Christ Jesus is in this book. Several men and women are trying to neutralize the Second Coming of Christ. Christ has come once to this earth to die for us and guarantee eternal life with Him if we will only accept His offer. According to His own Revelation, Jesus will return only once more with His bride, the church. You may choose to ignore all this evidence that Jesus will only come to earth one more time and that He will not come as two phases of His one coming.

The book of Revelation aligns itself with the words of Christ throughout the New Testament. The book stands alone as the pure book of the end times of this world. It is very clear as to the resurrection and the Second Coming of Christ. Please do not take one part of Scripture and fall into the trap of making up theories that somehow puts you in a special place with Christ. Millions of the followers of Christ have suffered terrible torment and even beheadings for their belief in our Savior. Be very cautious when accepting one man's theory because you do not want to put the effort into studying the subject for yourself. That includes my words to you in this commentary. Read the whole text of the Revelation, then go back to these other prophetic Scriptures and see how they match up to the perfect picture of the return of Jesus in the clouds.

Read – Chapter 22:20-21

Here John puts his two-cents in by asking the Lord to return to His own soon. Are you ready to see Jesus? Paradise is full of those who have gone on before us that knew Jesus and confessed His name. Hades, too, is full of those who rejected Jesus while here on earth. If you know Jesus as your Savior, you will not experience the second death. You will be one of millions who will eat from the Trees of Life along with the angels of God and His Son.

If you are still rejecting the salvation offered to you, then you will experience the second death where you will find yourself alone in a sea of burning sulfur. You will hear the pain of others, but never see them. I believe you will be able to see the glory of the New Jerusalem and your family, but be unable to communicate with them. That will be a torture worse than the sulfur fire itself.

What you have just read in this commentary shows you the complete picture of the Second Coming of Christ. Nowhere in the Bible or this book of Revelation have we found one verse telling us of a "Two Phase" return to earth to accept His church. There is no doubt that many of you who have been indoctrinated will change your mind and follow the road Jesus had laid out for you. My only prayer can be that when the time comes and the antichrist appears, you will run like the wind away from him and remember what you have learned in this study.

APPENDIX A

The Vision of Margaret Macdonald

(1830)

What you are about to read is a shocking story as told by a teenage girl that would change man's interpretation of the word of God in a very dangerous way. This young girl would be a servant of Satan as she told her story. Margaret was the last in her family to accept Jesus as her Savior. Many people investigated Margaret after her testimony of a vision of Jesus came to her as she was in a trance. Margaret had been ill and bedridden for a couple of years when this vision appeared. At first, she thought that the vision was evil, but after a time she concluded that this vision was from God. It involved a coming of Christ for two different groups of Christian people. The first was a group who was considered to be in the Spirit and the second was a group of Christians considered not filled with the Spirit.

Margaret came up with a theory of the Coming of Christ. Her vision told her that there would be a one time coming for the Spirit filled Christians that would be in secret and Jesus would only be seen by these Believers. The other set of Believers considered to be without the Spirit would go through the Tribulation and then be a part of the Second Coming of Christ that would be considered a public affair. The measure of who had the Holy Spirit and who did not was who spoke in tongues and who did not.

She gave some examples of her vision about Biblical passages. One of those was the case of two men in the field, "one would be taken, and the other left." The one taken was the man filled with the Holy Spirit; the one who stayed would go over into the Tribulation and he would do that without the benefit of having the Spirit with him.

Related Verse(s) / Matthew 24:40-41...*Two men will be in the field; one will be taken and the other left. Two women will be grinding with a hand mill; one will be taken and the other left.*

When Matthew 24:30-31 speaks of the "sign of the Son of God appearing in the sky:" the part of the same verse tells us "they will see" the son of Man coming on the clouds; what exactly is that "sign?" Margaret said that the "they" in this verse refers to only those Believers that are filled with the Spirit. The next part of the verse is problematic for her vision when comparing to the next verse that says, "And He will send His angels with a loud trumpet call." The noise this trumpet will make will only be heard by those being caught up with Jesus in the clouds, according to Margaret. Now Margaret is in real trouble again when explaining why Jesus will send His angels from one end of the world to the other to harvest (or gather) His elect. The elect refers to ALL His family.

Actually, this theory implies that there is a "split coming" of Christ. That is to say that only part of the church will go to heaven before the Tribulation, the balance will have to stay back and I guess be the Believers who have been given the task of preaching the Gospel. This thought defeats all reasonable thinking and is opposite to what Christ has told us.

Her vision was picked up by other religious leaders, which resulted in heresy being preached and taught in many churches even up to this very day.

Related Verse(s) / *I Thessalonians 4:16-18...For the Lord himself will come down from heaven, with a loud command, with the voice of the archangel and with the trumpet call of God, and the dead in Christ will rise first. After that, we who are still alive and are left will be caught up together with them in the clouds to meet the Lord in the air. And so we will be with the Lord forever. Therefore encourage each other with these words.*

I have a very hard time squaring her vision with some sort of clandestine meeting in the air with Christ. That would mean that only some Believers could hear it and others Believers could not. Those who do not know Christ Jesus must not be able to hear the noise either.

Let's look at another set of verses along these same lines. The verses below tell us that the Second Coming of Christ will not come until the antichrist is revealed. There will be no question of who he is to the churches. If we were to believe the vision of Margaret Macdonald, we would be calling this the Third Coming of Jesus, and she in fact is calling Jesus a liar as He explains exactly how He will return for His church.

Related Verse(s) / *II Thessalonians 2:3-4…Don't let anyone deceive you in any way, for that day will not come until the rebellion occurs and the man of lawlessness is revealed, the man doomed to destruction. He will oppose and will exalt himself over everything that is called God or is worshiped, so that he sets himself up in God's temple, proclaiming himself to be God.*

Now we could spend many hours talking about the development of this "Any Time Now" theory brought about by a very ill teenager who admits that what she sees at first seems evil. We could speak of men like John Norton, J. N. Darby, and others who scrambled to take authorship of this poor girl's theory, but there is not enough room in this book to tell the story. Both of these men have written extensively about this very unusual coming of our Savior.

All this comes down to is this: Are you ready to hang your hat on a theory that can be traced back to 1830, or are you ready to count on what Jesus is saying to you in His Revelation of His Coming?

I have a very hard time squaring her vision with some sort of clandestine meeting in the air with Christ. That would mean that only some Believers could hear it and others Believers could not. Those who do not know Christ Jesus must not be able to hear the noise either.

Let's look at another set of verses along these same lines. The verses below tell us that the Second Coming of Christ will not come until the antichrist is revealed. There will be no question of who he is to the churches. If we were to believe the vision of Margaret Macdonald, we would be calling this the Third Coming of Jesus, and she in fact is calling Jesus a liar as He explains exactly how He will return for His church.

Related Verse(s) / *II Thessalonians 2:3-4…Don't let anyone deceive you in any way, for that day will not come until the rebellion occurs and the man of lawlessness is revealed, the man doomed to destruction. He will oppose and will exalt himself over everything that is called God or is worshiped, so that he sets himself up in God's temple, proclaiming himself to be God.*

Now we could spend many hours talking about the development of this "Any Time Now" theory brought about by a very ill teenager who admits that what she sees at first seems evil. We could speak of men like John Norton, J. N. Darby, and others who scrambled to take authorship of this poor girl's theory, but there is not enough room in this book to tell the story. Both of these men have written extensively about this very unusual coming of our Savior.

All this comes down to is this: Are you ready to hang your hat on a theory that can be traced back to the year of 1830, or are you ready to count on what Jesus is saying to you in His Revelation of His Coming?

The following is a copy of the handwritten account of a vision Margaret Macdonald, a young teenage Scottish girl, had while spending months being very ill. This is being reproduced from a book titled, The Rapture Event by Dave MacPherson (1990) pp. 149-152.

THE FOLLOWING SECTION HAS NOT BEEN EDITED AND WAS PRINTED AS GIVEN TO US IN Dave MacPherson's BOOK LISTED IN THE PREVIOUS PARAGRAPH.

THIS LETTER WAS WRITTEN IN THE YEAR OF 1830.

"It was <u>first</u> the <u>awful state</u> <u>of the land</u> that was pressed upon me. I saw the blindness and infatuation of the people to be very great. I felt the cry of Liberty just to be the <u>hiss of the serpent</u>, to drown them in perdition. It was just 'no God.' I repeated the words, now there is distress of the nations, with perplexity, the seas and the waves roaring, men's hearts failing them for fear- now look out for the sign of the Son of man. Here I was made to stop and cry out, O it is not known what the sign of the Son of man is; the people of God think they are waiting, but they know not what it is. <u>I felt</u> this needed to be revealed, and <u>that there was a great darkness and error about it</u>; but suddenly what it was burst upon me with a glorious light. I saw it was just the Lord himself descending from heaven with a shout, just the glorified man, even Jesus; but that all must, as Steven was, be filled with the Holy Ghost, that they might look up, and see the brightness of the Father's glory. I saw the error to be, that men think it will be something seen by the natural eye; but 'tis spiritual discernment that is needed, the eye of God in his people. Many passages were revealed, in a light in which I had not before seen them. I repeated, "Now is the kingdom of Heaven like unto ten virgins, who went forth to meet the Bridegroom, five wise and five foolish; they that were foolish took their lamps, but took no oil with them; but they that were wise took oil in their vessels with their lamps." "But be ye not unwise, but understanding what the will of the Lord is; and be not drunk with wine wherein is excess, but be filled with the Spirit." This was the oil the wise virgins took in their vessels-this is the light to be kept burning-the light of God-that we may discern that which cometh not with observation to the natural eye. Only those who have the light of God within them will see the sign of his appearance. No need to follow them who say, see here, or see there, for this day shall be as the lightening to those in whom the living Christ is. Tis Christ in us that will lift us up-he is the light-tis only those that are alive in him that will be caught up to meet him in the air. I saw that we must be in the Spirit, when he saw a throne set in heaven-but I

saw that the glory of the ministration of the Spirit had not been known. I repeated frequently, but the spiritual temple must and shall be reared, and the fullness of Christ be poured into his body, and then shall we be caught up to meet him. Oh none will be counted worthy of this calling but his body, which is the church, and which must be a candlestick all of gold. I often said, Oh the glorious inbreaking of God which is now about to burst on this earth; Oh the glorious temple which is now about to be reared, the bride adorned for her husband; and what a holy, holy bride she must be, to be prepared for such a glorious bridegroom. I said, Now shall the people of God have to do with realities-now shall the glorious mystery of God in our nature be known-now shall it be known what it is for man to be glorified. I felt that the revelation of Jesus Christ has yet to be opened up-it is not knowledge of God that contains, but it is an entering into God-I saw that there was a glorious breaking in of God to be. I felt as Elijah, surrounded with chariots of fire.

I saw as it were, the spiritual temple reared, and the Head Stone brought forth with shoutings of grace, grace, unto it. It was a glorious light above the brightness of the sun, that shone around me. I felt that those who were filled with the Spirit, could see spiritual things, and feel walking in the midst of them, while those who had not the Spirit could see nothing- so that two shall be in one bed, the one be taken and the other left, because on has the light of God within while the other cannot see the Kingdom of Heaven. I saw the people of God in an awful situation, surrounded by nets and entanglements, about to be tried, and many about to be deceived and fall. Now will THE WICKED be revealed, with all the power and signs and lying wonders, so that if it were possible the very elect will be deceived-This is the fiery trial which is to try us. It will be for the purging and purifying of the real members of the body of Jesus; but Oh it will be a fiery trial. Every soul will be shaken to the very enter. The enemy will try to shake in every thing we have believed-but the trial of real faith will be found to honour and praise and glory. Nothing but what is of God will stand. The stony-ground hearers will be made manifest- the love of many will wax cold. I frequently said that night, and often since, now shall the awful sight of a false Christ be seen on this earth, and nothing but the living Christ in us can detect this unusual attempt of the enemy to deceive-for it is with all deceivableness of unrighteousness he will work-he will have a counterpart for every part of God's truth, and an imitation for every work of the Spirit. The Spirit must and will be poured out on the church, that she may be purified and filled with God-and just in proportion as the Spirit of God works, so will he-when our Lord anoints men with power, so will he. This is particularly the nature of the trial, though which those are to pass who will be counted worthy to stand before the Son of Man. There will be outward trial too, but 'tis principally temptation. It is brought on by the outpouring if the Spirit, and will just increase in proportion as the Spirit is poured out. The trial of the church is from antichrist. It is being filled by the Spirit that we shall be kept. I frequently said, O be filled with the Spirit-have the light of God in you, that you may detect Satan-be full of eyes within-be clay in the hands of the potter-submit to be filled, filled with God. This will build the temple. It is not by might nor by power, but by my Spirit, saith the Lord. This will fit us to enter into the marriage supper of the Lamb. I saw it to be the will of God that all should be filled. But what hindered the real life of God from being received by his people, was their turning from Jesus, who is the way to the Father. They were not entering in by the door. For he is faithful who had said, by me if any man enter in he shall find pasture. They were passing the cross, through which every drop of the Spirit of God flows to us. All power that comes not through the blood of Christ is not of God. When I say, they are looking from the cross, I feel that there is much in it-they turn from the blood of the Lamb, by which we overcome, and in which our robes are washed and made white. There are low views of holiness, and a ceasing to condemn sin in the flesh, and a looking from him who humbled himself, and made himself of no reputation. Oh! It is needed, much needed at present, a leading back to the cross. I saw that night and often since, that there will be an outpouring of the Spirit on the body, such as has not been, a baptism of fire, that all the dross may be put away. Oh there must and will be such an indwelling of the living God as has not been-the servants of God sealed in their foreheads-great conformity to Jesus-his holy image seen in his people-just the bride made comely, by his comeliness put upon her. This is what we are at present made to pray much for, that speedily we may all be made ready to meet our Lord in the trial, though which those are to pass who will be counted worthy to stand before the Son of Man. There will be outward trial too, but 'tis principally temptation. It is brought on by the outpouring if the Spirit, and will just increase in proportion as the Spirit is poured out. The trial of the church is from antichrist. It is being filled by the Spirit that we shall be kept. I frequently said, O be filled with the Spirit-have the light of God in you, that you may detect Satan-be full of eyes within-be clay in the hands of the potter-submit to be filled, filled with God. This will build the temple. It is not by might nor by power, but by my Spirit, saith the Lord. This will fit us to enter into the marriage supper of the Lamb. I saw it to be the will of God that all should be filled. But what hindered the real life of God from being received by his people, was their turning from Jesus, who is the way to the Father. They were not entering in by the door. For he is faithful who had said, by me if any man enter in he shall find pasture. They were passing the cross, through which every drop of the Spirit of God flows to us. All power that comes not through the blood of Christ is not of God. When I say, they are looking from the cross, I feel that there is much in it-they turn from the blood of the Lamb, by which we overcome, and in which our robes are washed and made white. There are low views of holiness, and a ceasing to condemn sin in the flesh, and a looking from him who humbled himself, and made himself of no reputation. Oh! It is needed, much needed at present, a leading back to the cross. I saw that night and often since, that there will be an outpouring of the Spirit on the body, such as has not been, a baptism of fire, that all the dross may be put away. Oh there must and will be such an indwelling of the living God as has not been-the servants of God sealed in their foreheads- great conformity to Jesus-his holy image seen in his people- just the bride made comely, by his comeliness put upon her. This is what we are at present made to pray much for, that speedily we may all be made ready to meet our Lord in the air-and it will be. Jesus wants his bride. His desire is toward us. He that shall come, will come, and will not tarry. Amen and Amen. Even so come Lord Jesus."

It is very difficult to put any confidence in this statement by Ms. Macdonald as a basis for the unusual acceptance of a Pre-Tribulation Rapture theory considering what has been written here. No matter who may read this letter, I have yet to hear the Biblical foundation for the assumption that it has caused.

You will notice that in the first lines of this letter, we read about what she believes to be an evil vision. It is only after taking a few liberties with Scripture that her "Anytime Now" theory has any merit. If we follow this letter even further, we see it in the hands of several church leaders of various denominations, i.e. the Brethren, the Catholic Apostolic Church, and men like Edward Irving and John Darby. I would go into this more deeply, but it would take another book to describe the astonishing cover-up of the genesis of the Pre-Tribulation Rapture movement. This type of deception is exactly why we need to read our Bibles and make all spiritual leaders prove what they are saying.

There have been many men and women over the years that have taught the theory of a Pre-Tribulation Rapture. It certainly sounds wonderful, but it has not one single fact of Scripture behind it. Oh yes, they give bits and pieces of Biblical text, but it always requires a faith level that goes well beyond Biblical faith. They are like others who feel that there is no God, and believe that this earth was created by itself over an unverifiable time span. If all Christians were to have the faith level of some of these atheists, they would set this earth on fire for the Lord. The message of the Scripture that you have read here is dead serious. Please do not take a chance and end up in hell because you were afraid to investigate what Jesus has said.

QUESTIONS

If you have any questions about this study in Revelation, please write, call, or e-mail me at the addresses below. If you do not agree with what I have written, please write me explaining in detail by the use of Scripture where I am wrong.

My goal is to get every Believer to read and study the Book of Revelation carefully and read it through many times. Billions of people over the centuries have been taught theories that cannot withstand scrutiny, and as a result, are now in Hades or headed in that direction today. If just one of you who read this material will act on what you have read, and have received the peace that only the Holy Spirit can give on the subject of the return of Christ for His church, I will have completed my task with joy.

Pastor J. R. Bushong
SonLife Ministries
P.O. Box 404
434-249-8395
Lovingston, VA 22949
bushongjim@aol.com

REFERENCES

Brand, C., Draper, C. & England, A. (2003). Holman illustrated Bible dictionary. Nashville, TN: Holman Bible Publishers.

Lahaye, T. & Ice, T. (2001). *Charting the end times: a visual guide to understanding Bible prophecy.* Eugene, OR: Harvest House Publishers.

MacPherson, D. (1980). *The incredible cover-up.* Medford, OR: Omega Publications.

MacPherson, D. (1983). *The great rapture hoax.* Fletcher, NC: New Puritan Library.

MacPherson, D. (1995). *The rapture plot.* Simpsonville, SC: Millennium III Publishers.

McKeever, J.M. (1978). *Christians will go through the tribulation and how to prepare for it.* Medford, OR: Alpha Omega Publishing Company.

Overstreet, B.E. (n.d.) *Will the Christian go through the great tribulation?* Jackson, MS: Self-published.

Rudolf, J.C. (November 24, 2010). *World "dangerously close" to food crisis,*

U.N. says. Green: A Blog About Energy and the Environment. New York: New York Times.

Towns, E.L. (2001). *Theology for today.* Ft. Worth, TX: Harcourt Publishers.